PILLARS for Christian Mentoring

Dr. Latanya Hughes

CreateSpace

A Division of On-Demand Publishing, LLC.

www.createspace.com

Copyright © 2014 by Dr. Latanya Hughes

All rights reserved. No portion of this book may be reproduced, stored in a retrieval system, or transmitted in any form or by any means – electronic, mechanical, photocopy, recording, scanning, or other – except for brief quotations in critical reviews or articles, without the prior written permission of the publisher.

ISBN: 1502558254
ISBN-13: 978-1502558251

Library of Congress Control Number: 2015909937
CreateSpace Independent Publishing Platform
North Charleston, SC

Printed in the United States of America

DEDICATED TO EVERY PERSON SEEKING TO IMPROVE THEIR LIFE AND TO THOSE WHO FEEL NEGLECTED, FORGOTTEN, AND OVERLOOKED.

Table of Contents

Introduction 1
Mentoring 17
The Role of the Mentor 28
Choosing a Mentor 121
PILLAR 131
The Premature Stage 144
The Infant Stage 163
The Learning Stage 170
The Living Stage 177
The Assessment Stage 182
The Rebuilding Stage 214
Mentoring and Organizations 221
What's Next? 239
Glossary 249
Bibliography 254

Acknowledgements

I thank God the Father, God the Son, and God the Holy Spirit who always causes me to triumph. When the wicked, even my enemies, came against me to eat up my flesh, they stumbled and fell. What they meant for evil, God turned it around for my good! For this reason, I am completely convinced that nothing shall ever separate me from the love of God. I stand firmly on Jeremiah 29: 11-14. It encourages me and reminds me when I feel alone and lost, I am not. God is always thinking about me and has something great in store for me. He always wants to do me good!

To my editor, Melanie Endsley-Francisco: THANK YOU! God reconnected us at the appropriate time. I appreciate your candor and flexibility. You pushed me, challenged me, and opened my eyes to possibilities I honestly likely would not have conceived on my own.

I am so grateful for my mother, Prophet Dr. Karen E McCray. When I think of a smidgeon of what my mother has done for me, I cannot thank her enough. She has been the best support system I could ever ask or hope for. I only pray I can leave a legacy in this Earth she is Godly proud of and one that will speak to her strength and the lessons she has taught her children. She has taught me the importance of prayer and how to pray. She is more than my mother. She is my friend!

What can I say about my sister, Michele Johnson? Growing up I did not like my sister. I thought she was a goody two-shoes. Today, you can't say anything bad about her around me. I think it is the nature of siblings to be at odds with each other. I was certainly on a completely different end of the spectrum from my sister. She is an introvert and I am definitely a social butterfly! BUT … My sister is my rock! She is a true intercessor and I am grateful for the fire she has sent up to The Lord on my behalf. She has read countless papers throughout my lifetime. Her attention for detail is second to none in my opinion. When it is all said and done, I admire my sister for her grace, her diligence, and her patience. She has mentored me in more ways than one, and she doesn't even know it!

To my prayer circle (DeVonne, LaTeaffia, Roger, Shená, and Vincent), you guys rock! You held up my arms for years and I am eternally grateful to you for it. You listened to me vent, cry, and scream. You screened calls and filtered people just so I could have the space and time to do what I needed to do. I could not ask for a better group of people. To you I say, "This is only the beginning. Let the flood begin!"

Introduction

> *Many moments of personal success and fulfillment in an individual's life come about through encouragement from someone else. ~ George Matthew Adams*

It is the 21st Century. Man has inhabited the Earth for millions of years. The most recent count of the world population is around 7,175,941,390 and counting. With so many people occupying space in the world, it is safe to say everyone is in need of guidance. At a June 2014 event at Jericho City of Praise in Maryland, Bishop T.D. Jakes answered the following question from Bishop Eugene Reeves: "When you are independent, where do you go for advice or counsel that you need?" Bishop Jakes responded, "Everyone needs a mentor and a role model." It is not a far reach to assert that many of us already know what a mentoring relationship is. We have a good idea of what it entails and why it is important. Notable author and leadership expert John Maxwell believes when you engage in a mentoring relationship, you are raising someone up to a higher level and helping him or her be successful.[1]

Mentoring has been around for centuries. Much of the research will tell you mentoring began with the Greek philosopher Homer in his tale, *Odyssey*. In this tale, the Goddess Athene disguises herself and takes Odysseus' son on a developmental journey in order to maintain the Kingdom of Ithaca and to develop a successor to the throne. Truthfully, we can trace the concept of mentoring further than this to Biblical times.

By definition, a "mentor" is someone who teaches or gives help and advice to a less experienced and often younger person. This person is a trusted counselor or guide. In Hebrew, the word mentor is akin to the term *ya'ats* (yaw-ats); it means to advise, consult, give counsel, counsel, purpose, devise, or plan. The word *mentor* can also point to the Hebrew word *yadah* (yaw-daw') – to know, to cause to know, to teach. In the Greek, the word mentor points to *didaskalos* (did-as'-kal-os), which means one who is fitted to teach. Additionally, in the Greek, it points to the

---

[1] John Maxwell, *The Complete 101 Collection: What Every Leader Needs To Know* (Nashville, TN: Thomas Nelson, 2009), 308.

word *parakletos* (par-ak'-lay-tos) – to counsel, assist, advise, or support. There are other historic Biblical terms relating to mentoring (the act of teaching and/or counseling others). Understanding how old the practice of mentoring actually is, we can point to specific examples of mentors in the Bible. For instance, below are a few notable Biblical mentoring relationships.

- Jethro and Moses
- Moses and Joshua
- Jesus and the disciples
- Paul and Timothy
- Paul and Titus

Scripture provides us with clear instructions regarding mentoring. Titus 2:3-5[2] declares,

> Older women likewise are to be reverent in behavior, not slaves to much wine. They are to teach what is good, and so train the young women to love their husbands and children, to be self-controlled, pure, working at home, kind, and submissive to their own husbands, that the word of God may not be reviled.

Other points in Scripture regarding mentoring include 1 Peter 5:5, which declares, "In the same way, you younger

---
[2] English Standard Version, ESV

men, be subject to the elders." Moreover, Titus 2:2, 6-8[3] points to a similar expression:

> Older men are to be level headed, worthy of respect, sensible, and sound in faith, love, and endurance ... In the same way, encourage the young men to be self-controlled in everything. Make yourself an example of good works with integrity and dignity in your teaching. Your message is to be sound beyond reproach, so that the opponent will be ashamed, having nothing bad to say about us.

The recording of these Scriptures and the notable mentoring relationships in the Bible lets us know the importance of relationship and instruction. When Jesus mentored the disciples, he did so in a number of ways – primarily through parables and deeds. He often shared with them His position and how He was the Chief Cornerstone (see Matthew 21:42) by which the Church would be built upon. As such, Jesus had to be the example – the model - the disciples used as they fulfilled the Great Commission as outlined in Matthew 28:19-20 to "go, make disciples of all nations, baptizing them in the name of the Father and of the Son and of the Holy Spirit, teaching them

---

[3] Holman Christian Standard Bible, HCSB

to observe everything I have commanded you. And remember, I am with you always, to the end of the age."

With all of these historic, Biblical references of mentoring, you may be wondering if there are any modern-day representations. Of course there are! Some modern examples of mentoring relationships include:

- Aquaman and Aqualad
- Batman and Robin
- The Karate Kid (Pat Morita & Ralph Macchio)
- Ip Man and Bruce Lee
- Yoda and Luke Skywalker

While most of these examples are works of fiction, they are absolutely applicable. Anyone can relate to these examples – from the cartoon enthusiast to the sci-fi lover. Pointing to real-life examples, we can look at Martin Luther King, Jr., Gandhi, or Nelson Mandela and their influence on others. These visual representations serve as a point of reference. As we embark on this journey towards mentoring, keep these examples in mind. They will help you, whether you are the mentor or the protégé.

If you are the mentor, it is important to remember that you serve as a cornerstone, a PILLAR, a support system for the person or people you are mentoring. You are a structural foundation to help build said individual(s). With this in mind, the stages of the mentoring relationship in this book are likened to a pillar. Each stage of the relationship is defined in detail with examples and

When Jesus mentored the disciples, he did so in a number of ways – primarily through parables and deeds.

recommendations on how to navigate successfully through them. It will also reveal limitations to the model as we recognize the unknown attributes of people and their unpredictable nature. Before diving into the model, the distinction between mentoring and coaching, which is easily confused quite often, will be clarified. It is also necessary to discuss the two types of mentoring relationships: informal and formal. Moreover, it is important to note that mentoring can benefit individuals and organizations as it relates to leadership development.

Personal Story

I was always an impressionable person, even from when I was a child. My mother would tell me, "Latanya, you are too gullible. You are too trusting. There are some things, my dear child, you need to learn about yourself and more importantly other people." I did not understand what she meant at the time. Indeed, I was a very trusting person. I was the complete opposite of both my parents and my sister. I would sometimes blindly follow the crowd. Other times, I would do my own thing, at times to my own detriment. One thing was certain: I needed proper guidance.

While attending Lincoln Elementary in Riviera Beach, Florida, I had a teacher named Mrs. Burke who would always speak positively to me. She would always encourage her students and push them to their maximum potential. Mrs. Burke took extra care with students who were gifted. She was the reason I was so passionate about attending Tuskegee University. She would always talk so highly about it. She always said it was the best experience of her life! Mrs. Burke not only encouraged her students, she had a knack for pulling out the best in us. When she saw we were gifted in a particular area, she reinforced it. She made sure we knew how great we were at it. I looked up to Mrs. Burke. I admired the way she carried herself and the way she spoke. I admired the way she interacted with us as students. I also admired her passion. She was active not only in the school system but in the community as well. Next to my mother and maternal grandmother, Mrs. Burke was one of my first informal mentors.

During my middle school years, my family moved to Charlotte, North Carolina. There I attended Smith Middle School and met a shop teacher named Mr. Colson. Everyone looked at me as if I was strange when I enrolled in his class. I turned out to be one of his best students. I loved his class. I would spend most of my free time with him. He took me under his wing and taught me a lot about woodworking. It wasn't about the wood or crafting the piece. It was the precision. He taught me how to be patient and take pride in my work. He was like that with any student who showed potential. If you took the class because you were genuinely interested in it and not because you thought it was an easy "A" course, he knew it. If he saw you had an eye for detail or was able to design a piece, he would encourage it. At the end of the year, all of our pieces were on display at the graduation ceremony. Eventually, I worked with Mr. Colson to make an entertainment cabinet for my parents. My mother has it to this day. Mr. Colson was another informal mentor. Whenever I returned to Charlotte, my mother and I would look him and his lovely wife up and stop by the house to see them. They always took an interest in me and I never forgot it.

In my life, I had a number of informal and formal mentors. My experiences with my informal mentors have been so much better and have been more beneficial to me than my formal mentoring experiences. I have had formal mentors assigned to me in my professional career. Unfortunately, at some point or another in the relationship those mentors were more concerned with their own career paths. This left me to fend for myself, so to speak. I had to wing it quite frequently early in my career. Ultimately, I made many, many mistakes. In hindsight, I certainly would have done things much differently. The adage, "When you know better, you do better" comes to mind. I desperately wish I had known better. I could blame it on my age and lack of maturity; but, at the end of the day, it does not do me any good. What I can say is it has provided me with the experience and knowledge of an overcomer. The Bible declares in Romans 8:37,[4] "Yet in all these things we are more than conquerors through Him who loved us." Through it all, I am able to be transparent and share my passion for mentoring with others.

    One of the reasons I chose to create this mentoring model is because of my own experiences. I never want anyone to feel abandoned or the frustration of feeling lost and directionless. As I said before, I had mentors assigned to me early in my career, dating back to my undergraduate studies. Today,

Yet in all these things we are more than conquerors through Him who loved us.

I cannot tell you where some of them are or what they are doing. Others elected to be unresponsive when I reached out to them. If I knew then what I know now, I certainly would have done things much differently. I would have

---

[4] New King James Version, NKJV

spoken up for myself when some of these individuals were selected for me.

One thing we must realize as mentors is our role never truly ends. Rather, it evolves over time. In preparing to write this manuscript, I spoke with a number of people either who are in mentoring relationships or have been in mentoring relationships in the past. One consistent theme emerged: the timeframe or span of the mentoring relationship. No one could quite express how long the relationship should last. What I did infer from a few of the conversations was the majority of people are disappointed in their mentoring relationships. After a period of time, the relationship lacked substance and some found themselves in a similar predicament as me: without a mentor.

The Value of this Book

The premise of this book is to bring clarity about the tenure of the mentoring relationship in addition to its phases. The intent is to provide a means of identifying at which phase of the mentoring relationship you are in from a Christian perspective. It has been interesting and quite fun gathering my thoughts and pulling research to develop this model, which is an expansion of work done by Kathy Kram. I am excited to see how this concept will help shape Christian mentoring relationships in the future – from both an individual and organizational perspective.

While this book is written from a Christian perspective, you do not have to be a Christian for the principles and concepts to apply. Since mentoring dates back to early Biblical times (as discussed earlier in the book), it is a good foundation to build upon. I am a Christian and believe in the death, burial, and resurrection of Jesus Christ. I believe there is a reason for everything under heaven, and I believe God gives us instructions on how to maneuver through life on this Earth. It is His will that we live an abundant life. The Bible is full of instruction and examples on everything from leadership to legal situations. It is a precedent for many things. As such, it is a precedent for this book.

In my mind, mentoring is like a parent-child relationship. It ends when one of you draws your last breath. In the beginning, as you will see, there will be a lot of attention given as well as hands-on experience. Over time, as the protégé matures and achieves certain milestones, the mentor's personal one-on-one involvement shifts. When a child grows and develops, the responsibilities of the parent towards the child shifts. The parent makes the necessary adjustments to ensure the child grows and matures satisfactorily. When the child becomes a teenager, the parent is not still spoon-feeding them nor are they changing their diapers. However, the parent's responsibilities towards the child shifts and their focus may be more on the child's emotional and social well-being during their teenage years; whereas in their infant and toddler years, it is more on their biological needs.

As a mentor, you will shift your focus as your relationship with your protégé evolves. What your protégé needs from you in the beginning of the relationship may not necessarily be what they need from you in the middle. Once you reach certain milestones in the relationship, you build and you keep building. You build until you cannot build any more. Then at that point, you find something else in the protégé's life to build.

When exploring ideas governing growth and development, consider the concept that people's thoughts influence their feelings and behavior, which subsequently influences their performance. For example, parents take the time to develop their child's self-esteem in their developmental years, so they have a high likelihood of success. William Watson Purkey talks about Goldberg's argument that underachievers are generally less confident and less ambitious while Shaw and Alves say underachievers are less self-accepting.[5] Durr and Schmatz contribute to the discussion and state underachievers lack a sense of personal worth.[6] Dr. Ranjit Singh Malhi says[7], "Research also shows that feeling worthless can be depressing and depression generally inhibits performance."[8] He goes on to

People who feel worthy, able, and competent are more likely to achieve their goals than those who feel worthless, impotent, and incompetent.

---

[5] William Watson Purkey, *Self-Concept and School Achievement* (Englewood Cliffs, New Jersey: Prentice-Hall, Inc., 1970), 20-21.
[6] Ibid
[7] Dr. Malhi cites several sources to include Battle (1990), Bhatti (1992), and Hokanson, Rubert, wElker, Hollander, and Hedeen (1989).
[8] Ranjit S. Malhi, (2010). "Self-Esteem and Peak Performance At Work," *TQM Consultants*, Retrieved from http://www.tqm.com.my/web/05_bookArticle_09.html

cite work by Mark R. Leary and Deborah L. Downs: "People who feel worthy, able, and competent are more likely to achieve their goals than those who feel worthless, impotent, and incompetent."[9] People with a high self-esteem and high self-concept tend to be more successful at achieving their goals. Thus, people with high self-esteem and self-concept are what organizations seek. Organizations also seek people who can influence positive self-concept and behavior in others. This process, along with other learning models, occurs in stages. As such, my PILLAR model occurs in stages.

Who Will Benefit from This Book?

While it may seem obvious to you who will benefit from reading this book, others may not find it so obvious. You are reading it, because something about the title or the description of the book caught your attention. Mentoring is a hot topic in leadership development, and I suspect it will continue to be for many more years. People are interested in self-help and self-development. While I do not like to segregate anyone, and it certainly is not my intent to leave

---

[9] Ibid

anyone out, this book will be beneficial to anyone interested in personal development. Whether you are a leader, follower, or human resources professional, this book is for you! Let us begin our journey …

Mentoring

> *What I've found about it is that there are some folks you can talk to until you're blue in the face – they're never going to get it and they're never going to change. But every once in a while, you'll run into someone who is eager to listen, eager to learn, and willing to try new things. Those are the people we need to reach. We have a responsibility as parents, older people, teachers, people in the neighborhood to recognize that. ~ Tyler Perry*

It has already been established that mentoring is nothing new. However, a relatively new concept, coaching, has blurred the lines a bit. Why do I say coaching is relatively new? Considering mentoring dates back to Biblical times and coaching has only been on the scene since the early 1800's, it is a relatively new concept. Consequently, it is important to allot some time to discuss a few distinct differences between mentoring and coaching.

Mentoring versus Coaching

Let us first understand what is coaching and how long it has been around. The International Coach

Federation defines coaching as "partnering with clients in a thought-provoking and creative process that inspires them to maximize their personal and professional potential."[10] There are different types of coaching services available from business coaching to life skills. Organizations are beginning to invest in coaching services; some believe if they allocate resources to their human capital, they will experience an increase in productivity and the overall success of the organization will improve. This is business coaching. Historically, it is argued the term "coach" was slang for an Oxford University tutor who "carried" a student through an exam. Later, the term was used to define someone who improved the performance of athletes.[11] Dating to the early 1930s, research studies into business coaching began with sales teams.[12]

---

[10] "What Is Professional Coaching?" *International Coach Federation*, accessed April 14, 2014, http://www.coachfederation.org/need/landing.cfm?ItemNumber=978andnavItemNumber=567

[11] Elaine Cox, Tatiana Bachkirova and David Clutterbuck, *The Complete Handbook of Coaching,* 2nd Ed, (Sage Publication), 2014.

[12] "How Did Business Coaching Get Started?" *Worldwide Association of Business Coaches,* accessed April 14, 2014, http://www.wabccoaches.com/faqs.htm

Often people tend to equate mentoring with coaching. In fact, the two are not the same. While a mentor may be a coach, a coach may not be a mentor. The primary difference is mentoring is relational and focuses on long-term goals whereas coaching focuses on immediate problems.[13] Most mentoring relationships last *at least one year* while coaching relationships last about 3 months. Coaching relationships, however, can last up to a year. Coaching relationships focus primarily on performance and are more functional and task-oriented. Contrastingly, even though mentoring relationships tend to be more personal, they can be professional as well.

Consider sports coaching for a moment. Sports coaches are charged with providing guidance to their teams for a specified period. When the season ends, while the coach is still available, the nature of the relationship is "paused" until the season comes around again. Why is this so? The need for the coach and the players has resurfaced. The central purpose for the parties coming together is evident. Prior to the start of the new season, the coach and

---

[13] Harvard Business Essentials, *Coaching and Mentoring* (Harvard Business Press Books), 2004.

the players come together to perform pre-season drills. They review tapes of games of their opponents to strategize for the upcoming season.

Coaching – executive, leadership, business, and personal – is similar to this. The central purpose for the parties involved is evident. Even though the relationship may be short-term, the need for a coach may re-surface. The person soliciting the assistance of the coach may find another purpose. They may have another area where they feel the coach will be beneficial to them. Once that particular need has been addressed, like a sporting season, the relationship either ends or is on hiatus until the individual finds a need for the coach again. Now that the differences between mentoring and coaching have been discussed, let us look at the types of mentoring relationships.

Types of Mentoring Relationships

Mentoring relationships are all around us. People engage in mentoring relationships early in life. Although these relationships are not seen as such, they are what we call informal mentoring relationships. Think back to a time in your childhood where you looked up to someone. It could be a schoolteacher, a relative, a church member, or even someone from your community. Whoever that person was, you took advice from them. You looked to them as a model of how to behave, what decisions to make in certain situations, or even what to wear on certain occasions. These are informal mentoring relationships. These people poured into your life. It is akin to the old saying, "It takes a village to raise a child." Let us take a deeper look at informal mentoring relationships.

Informal Mentoring Relationships

I can remember when I was a little girl playing in my grandparent's backyard with my cousins. We had a number of favorite things to play, but our two favorite games were 'Red Light, Green Light' and 'Simon Says'. 'Simon Says' was my first taste of 'follow the leader' and often I would be frustrated by the game, at least until I got the hang of it. The rule of the game says you are not supposed to react or respond to anything the leader says unless it is preceded by, 'Simon says'. I have no idea who 'Simon' is, but when I first started playing the game, I did not like 'Simon'. He really got on my nerves. It was too confusing. However, the older I got and the more we played the game the better I became at following the leader.

I distinctly remember the best times we had playing 'Simon Says' was when our oldest (the 1st born in the family) cousin would come by to visit. He would come in the backyard and lead us in 'Red Light, Green Light', 'Simon Says', touch football, and basketball. Every single one of us looked up to him, because we believed in him. He was our superstar, hero cousin.

There is something to be said about the 'follow the leader' relationship. Most people are not following just anyone. People follow leaders they believe in. They follow leaders they can trust. More importantly, people follow leaders they consider to be examples. In his 2014 proclamation on mentoring, President Barack Obama declared,

> "Mentors help children build confidence, gain knowledge, and develop the strength of character to succeed inside and outside of the classroom. They are relatives, teachers, coaches, ministers, and neighbors. Anyone can be a mentor, and every child should have the chance to be a mentee."[14]

What the President shared is a reflection of what could be an informal or formal mentoring relationship. Informal mentors surround us. The nature of these relationships varies. What does an informal relationship look like?

In informal mentoring relationships, goals are unspecified and the outcomes of the relationship are unknown. Typically, the protégé selects the mentor, who may not have expert training. These relationships are normally long-term. Earlier I shared my personal story. The two relationships I highlighted – Mrs. Burke and Mr. Colson – were informal mentoring relationships. Informal relationships include those formed from family members, as the President indicated. Noticeably, parents and grandparents are informal mentors. However, many people

Our first experience with follow the leader relationships are in children's games like "Red Light, Green Light" and "Simon Says."

---

[14] Barack Obama, "Presidential Proclamation – National Mentoring Month, 2014," *White House,* December 31, 2013, http://www.whitehouse.gov/the-press-office/2013/12/31/presidential-proclamation-national-mentoring-month-2014

tend to overlook siblings, aunts, uncles, and even cousins as informal mentors.

In an organization, informal mentoring relationships develop frequently. Managers often look among their employees to see who has certain skills and abilities they can enhance for promotion opportunities. Other times, employees approach supervisors and managers to express their interest in improving so they can advance in the company. Now that we have a grasp on informal mentoring relationships, we need to turn our attention to formal mentoring relationships.

Formal Mentoring Relationships

Formal mentoring relationships are the opposite of informal mentoring relationships. These relationships tend to be professional in nature, but they can still be personal. In formal relationships, specific goals are targeted. Expectations and timelines are set to measure the effectiveness of the relationship. The timeline also ensures specific goals are met. If those goals are not met, the timeline addresses whether or not the allotted time was realistic. Additionally, the individuals involved are paired together strategically.

Formal mentoring includes group mentoring. This is where a group of individuals promotes the professional and/or personal development of its members with the assistance of a mentoring group leader. Most of the research about group mentoring focuses on youth and community development. However, the principle of group mentoring is beneficial to organizations as well. It promotes diversity, is efficient, and contributes to a vibrant culture.[15] With group mentoring, the focus is on multiple developments with less focus on personal development. Confidentiality is limited in this environment. Group mentoring highlights a number of attributes beneficial to the individuals involved. Some of the attributes include:

1. Peer support
2. Increased exposure to multiple levels of expertise and knowledge – each participant shares their own competencies with the group

---

[15] Lois Zachary, Ed.D., "Group Mentoring: Strategies for Success in Group Mentoring," humanresources.about.com/od/coachingmentoring/a/group_mentoring.htm

3. Participants are aware of issues related to ethnicity, sex, religion, etc. from the diverse perspectives in the group
4. More people can benefit from mentoring compared to one-on-one mentoring programs
5. Participants can enhance their learning and develop an understanding of how teams operate
6. Increased networking opportunities

The 21st Century has new terminology for mentoring. These include enterprise mentoring, people-first learning, and mentoring networks. According to Randy Emelo of ASTD,

> Enterprise mentoring is mentoring that is open to everyone in an organization. It is predicated on the belief that everyone has something to teach and everyone has something to learn. By opening up the practice of mentoring to all employees within an organization, companies can tap into deep pools of knowledge – often ones that have been previously overlooked. The large scale objective is to make the depth and breadth of all the knowledge in an organization available to all knowledge workers.[16]

Emelo goes on to define people-first learning as a process by which people look to connect with other people first

---

[16] Randy Emelo, "Conversations with Mentoring Leaders" [PDF document], *ASTD*, July 2011, p. 36.

when they have learning needs.[17] Finally, mentoring networks are learning networks created by the connections people make with colleagues when they are engaged in mentoring.[18]

Now that we have a deeper understanding of mentoring relationships, to include formal and informal, we can dive a little deeper. In the next chapter, we look at the role of the mentor. We see being a mentor is a PLUS, but it takes dedication and commitment. Let us continue …

---

[17] Ibid, p. 36
[18] Ibid, p. 36

The Role of the Mentor

> *Leaders should influence others in such a way that it builds people up, encourages and edifies them so they can duplicate this attitude in others. ~ Bob Goshen*

Becoming a mentor is a serious responsibility. It is not something to enter into lightly. The role of a mentor is to be supportive and to provide guidance as well as direction for the protégé. Warren Bennis is a noted leadership expert. Numerous people have pointed to his work on leadership, to include mentoring. Mia Gladstone argued one of Bennis' points on mentoring: "Mentors are trusted counselors or guides who provide direction toward a line of thought or inclination – developing personal concern and responsibility in assisting others."[19]

There are so many advantages to being a mentor. For instance, in a mentoring relationship, learning goes both ways. The mentor learns from the protégé as much as the

---

[19] Mia S. Gladstone, *Mentoring: A Strategy for Learning in a Rapidly Changing Society* (Montreal, Quebec: CEGEP John Abbot College, Research and Development Secretariat), 1988, p. 9

protégé learns from the mentor. What do I mean by this? The mentor will get a lot of insight from the protégé's background and history that may be beneficial to the mentor in their personal and professional development. It is also satisfying to help others. In doing so, you renew your own strength in your career and you improve your character. If the mentoring occurs formally in an organization, there is an opportunity to learn about different areas in the organization. The mentor's horizons broaden and new avenues of opportunities may be open. Moreover, the mentor's own skills sharpen. The mentor challenges and stretches their leadership skills, especially as the mentor engages with others from diverse backgrounds and generations. Last, mentors build legacies for themselves. Keeping this in mind, what are some key components a Christian leader must implement when engaging in a mentoring relationship? All of these things are a PLUS. PLUS is an acronym for Prayer, Listening, Understanding, and Servant. These are critical attributes Christian leaders must develop when mentoring others.

Prayer

Christian mentors must be rooted in PRAYER. Prayer *p*urposefully *r*eveals *a*lignment strategies for *y*ou in *e*very *r*eal situation. Prayer should be the foundation for mentoring endeavors. The Bible declares to us in Ephesians 6:18a,[20] "Pray at all times in the Spirit with every prayer and request." There is a direct relationship between prayer, God, and the function of the human brain. Dr. Andrew Newberg, Professor and Director of Research in the Myrna Brind Center of Integrative Medicine at Thomas Jefferson University and Hospital, proved this. "Our research indicates that our only way of comprehending God, asking questions about God, and experiencing God is through the brain."[21]

Christians model their lives and their Christian walk after Jesus. In everything, Jesus sought guidance from God through prayer. He said Himself in John 5:19,[22] "I assure you: The Son is not able to do anything on His own, but only what He sees the Father doing. For whatever the

---

[20] Holman Christian Standard Bible, HCSB
[21] Andrew Newberg, "Is God Only in Our Brain?" 2013, http://www.andrewnewberg.com/research/
[22] Holman Christian Standard Bible, HCSB

Father does, the Son also does these things in the same way." He modeled everything He did after God.

Without prayer, it is difficult to discern God's heart concerning the role of a mentor. Through prayer, the mentor receives God's instructions for how to move forward in the mentoring relationship. Through prayer, God reveals strategies to the mentor to align and / or realign the protégé (or the person serving as the mentor).

Prayer also expands the mentor's vision and opens the mentor's eyes to not only things in the physical realm but the spiritual. Dr. Newberg's study shows the importance of the temporal lobes of the brain in religious and spiritual experiences. "The amygdala and hippocampus have been shown to be particularly involved in the experience of visions, profound experiences, memory, and meditation."[23] In 2 Kings 6, Elisha the prophet prays to God to open the eyes of his servant so he (the servant) may see there were more with them than those who were against them. God honored Elisha's prayer and

---

[23] Andrew Newberg, "Do the Temporal Lobes Explain Religious Experiences?" 2013, http://www.andrewnewberg.com/research/

the eyes of his servant opened. Elisha's servant was afraid of Aram's army capturing them, but Elisha was confident. He had the assurance that God was on his side, but he was aware his servant did not have the same confidence or assurance. So he interceded.

Elisha's prayer life increased his discernment and connection with God. He saw things from multiple perspectives. As Christians lead and mentor others, they must be able to do the same. They must be confident and sure. They

PLUS — critical attributes Christian leaders must develop when mentoring others.

must be able to discern that which is spirit and that which is flesh. Moreover, they must be able to see from multiple angles. Christian leaders and mentors have to see a thing before it is known, meaning manifested in the Earth. This comes through prayer.

Recall earlier I stated one does not have to be a Christian for the principles in this book to work. Keeping this in mind, it is necessary to explore how prayer translates in different religions. According to the Encyclopedia of World Religions, Muslims perform ablutions before they pray. "As they pray, they assume a series of postures, such as standing, bowing, and prostration."[24] Some religions use external objects such as rosary beads in prayer. Others classify their prayers according to a specific purpose, to include losing weight.

Sigfried Gold is an atheist who prays morning, night, and before each meal. He started praying because of the 12-step program for food addiction he joined. Part of the program required participants to recognize God and to pray. After four years, "Gold is trim, far happier in his relationships and free of a lifelong ennui."[25] Gold still does not believe in God; however, he does believe in the power of *asking*. Ironically, Gold is not the only atheist who "believes" in the power of prayer. According to research on atheists by the Pew Research Center, 12% of Americans who say they do not believe in God and do not call themselves atheists pray. The research also indicates 26% of

---

[24] Robert S. Ellwood, and Gregory D. Alles, *Encyclopedia of World Religions*, Infobase Publishing, 2009: 348.

[25] Michelle Boorstein, "Some Nonbelievers Still Find Solace in Prayer," *The Washington Post*, June 24, 2013, http://www.washingtonpost.com/local/non-believers-say-their-prayers-to-no-one/2013/06/24/b7c8cf50-d915-11e2-a9f2-42ee3912ae0e_story.html

atheists consider themselves spiritual or religious and 14% believe in God or a universal spirit.[26]

Regardless of one's religious affiliation (or lack thereof), prayer is essential. It is the fundamental communication method between an individual and the deity they worship. Whether the person prays aloud, in their mind, by meditating, or by some other means of communication, prayer requires the individual to LISTEN.

Listening

Next to prayer, an important aspect of a mentor's role is LISTENING. Shena' Jordan is a Criminal Justice graduate of Virginia Union University in Richmond, Virginia. I asked her what she thought was the most important role of a leader. She said, "The most important role is to be a great listener." She went on to describe her relationship with her mentor. "My mentor listens to me without judging me or talking over me when I am trying to talk to them. They listen." I spoke with a youth praise dance leader about her selection to be a mentor. When I

---

[26] "Nones on the Rise: One in Five Adults Have No Religious Affiliation," *The Pew Research Center*, October 9, 2012, http://www.pewforum.org/files/2012/10/NonesOnTheRise-full.pdf

asked her what her expectations were of the relationship between her and the young woman she was mentoring, she responded, "I expect her to listen to me and take my advice." She went on to say, "The most important characteristic of being a leader is the ability to listen without judgment, speak the truth and not what the person wants to hear."

When listening, it is important to listen to understand not to respond. Mentors must practice active listening and engage in the conversation. The focus of attention is on what is said. There are four parts to active listening.

1. Seek to understand before seeking to be understood - this points back to listening to understand and not listening to respond. Here information is collected.

2. Be nonjudgmental – this requires a great deal of empathy.

3. Give your undivided attention to the speaker – there are many ways to show the speaker you are giving them your undivided attention. You can use eye contact (this can also be negative as it can be a sign of aggression, asserting dominance, or forcing submission) or you can speak through body language.

4. Use silence effectively – remember the adage, "Silence is golden?" This is true. So much can be learned when you listen and elect not to interrupt the speaker (unless it is absolutely necessary). This can be painful as people are so accustomed to talking. Enough positive feedback can be provided with body language or eye contact without using filler words like, "Uh huh, hmm, sure, and ok."

With listening, an easy way to approach it is by using the Golden Rule, "Do unto others as you would have them to do unto you." Think about how you would want someone to behave if you were speaking. Do you enjoy being interrupted? Do you like conversations where one person is domineering and providing little to no opportunity for anyone else to participate in the conversation? The point of listening is to understand what the other person has to say. How else will a mentor be able to make a connection with their protégé? If the mentor does not understand who their protégé is, what

The most important characteristic of being a leader is the ability to listen without judgment, speak the truth and not what the person wants to hear.

their passion is, or what their goals and aspirations are, how else will the mentor be able to take a vested interest in their protégé and show the protégé the mentor cares? How will the mentor be able to provide encouragement to the protégé? Listening leads to UNDERSTANDING.

Understanding

The Bible declares in Proverbs 4:7b,[27] "And in all your getting, get understanding." Understanding is essential. Not only must the mentor understand the protégé, but the protégé must also understand the mentor. This is how common ground is reached. What does it mean to understand? According to Merriam Webster, to understand means to know the meaning of (something, such as the words that someone is saying or a language), to know how (something) works or happens, to know how (someone) thinks, feels or behaves. Thus, without listening, there is no understanding.

Another important aspect of understanding is effective communication. Too often people take for granted the other person is following their logic. People speak and

---

[27] New King James Version

expect others to respond accordingly. What happens when the opposite occurs? Is it possible people are not communicating as effectively as they think? Effective communication occurs when the listener clearly and accurately *understands* what the speaker is saying and *feels* what the speaker is feeling.[28]

What happens when you mentor someone from a different culture than your own? Cross-cultural communication is important to understanding. How people think translates in the way they communicate. Different cultures communicate both verbally and through space and time. Geert Hofstede made pointed differences in the way people communicate in his cultural framework between high-context and low-context cultures. In non-technical language, think about adults and children. Adults represent high-context cultures and children represent low-context cultures. Low-context cultures require more attention; they need their hands held, so to speak. High-context cultures

---

[28] Steven K. Scott, *The Greatest Man Who Ever Lived: Secrets for Unparalleled Succes and Unshakable Happiness from the Life of Jesus* (New York, NY: Doubleday), 2009.

are more empowered and do not need as much hand holding.

When it comes to communication, leaders must keep in mind Hofstede's cultural framework. In his framework, there are several key insights that distinguish countries from each other: power distance, individualism vs. collectivism, masculinity vs. femininity, and uncertainty avoidance. With individualists, the preference is towards a loosely-knit social framework in which they are expected to take care of themselves and their immediate families only.[29] Collectivism represents a preference for a tightly-knit framework in society in which individuals can expect their relatives or members of a particular in-group to look after them in exchange for unquestioning loyalty.[30] Power distance affects communication, verbally and nonverbally. For example, there are distinct differences between Japanese and Korean communication.

> Perhaps the most elaborate verbal cues for power distance are the grammatical inflections found in such languages as Japanese and Korean. Japanese

---

[29] The Hofstede Centre. "National Cultural Dimensions," http://geert-hofstede.com/national-culture.html
[30] Ibid

has special word forms that show respect or reflect greater formality and politeness. Korean culture is strongly age sensitive, and an age difference of a year or less may require deferential language from the younger party. Two classes of inflections are used: honorific inflections to show respect to the persons mentioned, and no fewer than seven "speech levels" to show different degrees of respect to the listener.[31]

With respect to space and time, Hall identifies two types of people – monochronic and polychronic. Monochronic – "M" time – individuals are "sticklers" for time. Everything operates and functions according to a schedule. Contrarily, polychronic individuals prefer a higher degree of liberty.

Don't think because a person is chronically late they are being rude on purpose. It may be a cultural difference you need to address.

With polychronic individuals, there are multiple things happening at once. Typically low-context people are monochronic, and high-context people are polychronic.

---

[31] John Hooker, Cultural Differences in Business Communication, [PDF document], *Tepper School of Business*, 2008, http://ba.gsia.cmu.edu/jnh/businesscommunication.pdf

With the vast difference in cultures, there is bound to be a clash. This is true of low-context and high-context individuals as well as collectivists and individualists. As previously indicated, low-context individuals tend to be monochronic in nature whereas high-context individuals are polychronic. This may pose a problem, since a polychronic person may arrive chronically late to a meeting. The monochronic person may cringe at the thought and become irritated, believing the person is rude and does not honor time. This is not the case, since the flexibility afforded by the polychronic culture is embedded in the person's nature. If we were to examine collectivists and individualists, we would find "collectivists conform more to groups and are more cooperative than individualists."[32]

Other methods of communication affect how a message translates to others. People do not realize they communicate in many ways. Too often, people ignore what their body language is saying. In Western civilization,

---

[32] Smaranda Boros, Nicoleta Meslec, Petru L. Curseu, and Wilco Emons, "Struggles for Cooperation: Conflict Resolution Strategies in Multicultural Groups," *Journal of Managerial Psychology* 25, no. 5 (2010): 539-554, doi: 10.1108/02683941011048418.

people are in a hurry to go nowhere. Thus, Westerners come across as rude and devoid of value for other people. According to Psychology Today, "People are constantly throwing off a storm of signals. Microexpressions, hand gestures, and posture register almost immediately, a silent orchestra that can have long-lasting repercussions."[33] Body language is so important in business that Forbes printed an article about it: *10 Simple and Powerful Body Language Tips for 2013*.

 The way people communicate influences the way they think and represents who they are as well as their organizations, including the Church. When speaking, it is important to be aware of interference (anything that affects the meaning of the message). In an open conversation, Paul Dannar said, "Leaders are responsible not only for delivery of the message but also for ensuring the message is fully understood." Demographic traits also play a key role in communication. "Demographic traits can give us insight into our audience and allow for an audience-centered-approach that will make [us] more effective

---

[33] "Understanding body language," *Psychology Today*, http://www.psychologytoday.com/basics/body-language

communicators."[34] When it boils down to it, language shapes reality.

Servant

Last, mentors must be willing to SERVE. Jesus declares in Mark 9:35b,[35] "If anyone wants to be first, he must be last of all and servant of all." Bob Briner and Ray Pritchard wrote a book called, *The Leadership Lessons of Jesus*. In it, they talk about the importance of leaders taking care of their people. They note, "A leader takes care of his followers and those important to his followers. Those you are leading can only be effective when their needs *and* the needs of their families are met; an effective leader understands this and is sensitive to it."[36]

For the Lord corrects the one He loves, just as a father, the son he delights in.

There are benefits and rewards to serving. Christians do not serve to receive; however, it is always encouraging

---

[34] Scott McLean, *Business Communication for Success* (Irvington, NY: Flat World Knowledge, Inc.), 2010, 57

[35] Holman Christian Standard Bible, HCSB

[36] Bob Briner, and Ray Pritchard, (1997). *The Leadership Lessons Of Jesus* (Nashville, TN: Broadman and Holman Publishers), 1997, 27

to know there is a reward in store. A Christian's first reward is uniting with The Lord in heaven and hearing Him say, "Well done, thou good and faithful servant." Add to this, there are some 7500 promises in the Bible of God's faithfulness to reward His children. The New Living Translation denotes Hebrews 6:10, "For God is not unfair. How can he forget your hard work for Him, or forget the way you used to show your love for Him – and will do – by helping His children?"

Earlier I indicated the mentor looks at how they can help the person holistically. I also said part of mentoring is getting the person to understand who they are, which takes into account the person's social identity as well as their cultural beliefs and values. By grasping this information, the mentor can help the protégé network and make connections to help them achieve specific goals. It is not realistic for the mentor to assume they will be knowledgeable about everything the protégé needs. There will come moments in the relationship where the mentor will need to defer to someone else's expertise in a particular area. This does not mean the mentor is relinquishing their responsibilities as a mentor. It means the mentor is creating an opportunity for the protégé to expand their horizons and their network.

A mentor will not only provide their protégé with encouragement but the mentor will also correct their protégé when necessary. The correction is not to tear them down but to edify them in the same way God corrects us – with LOVE. Let us get a better understanding of what I mean by "Love." There are distinct differences between the types of love mentioned in the Bible: eros, phileo, and agape. Upon deeper examination, Dr. Bruce Winston discovered *agapao* (ag-ap-ah'-o). He notes this Greek word refers to a moral love, doing the right thing at the right time for the right reason. He goes on to say, "More specifically, *agapao* means to love in a social or moral sense, embracing the judgment and the deliberate assent of the will as a matter of principle, duty, and propriety."[37] What does all of this mean? *Agapao* love refers to how people show love to one another. This does not always translate to flowers and candy. It is not always the "niceties" of things showered

---

[37] Bruce Winston, *Be A Leader For God's Sake* (Virginia Beach, VA: School of Leadership Studies), 2002

upon each other. Sometimes love is shown through chastening (correction).

Proverbs 3:12[38] says, "For the Lord corrects the one He loves, just as a father, the son he delights in." When a mentor loves their protégé and corrects them in a manner that edifies them, the protégé's commitment to the relationship deepens. What does this look like? First, before the mentor administers discipline of any kind, the mentor must understand the situation. Often what appears on the surface is not what it really is. It is important to get to the root cause of the issue. Then you will know how to address the situation. Consider King Peggielene Bartels, the first lady king of Otuam,[39] who lives in the United States of America. In 2009, she received a call at 4:00 AM from a relative stating her uncle, the previous king, had passed away. The caller told her after performing the ritual, she was confirmed as the new king or "nana." Imagine being appointed the *first* female *king*. Imagine how the men in the

---

[38] New Living Translation
[39] Otuam is a small fishing village with approximately 7000 people on the coast of Ghana in Africa.

village felt! King Peggielene said, "If you step on my toes, I will hit you where it hurts."[40]

An obstacle King Peggielene Bartels has to overcome is the difference in time. The people in the village have no concept of the time difference. Therefore, she frequently received calls at 4:00 AM concerning disputes in the village. One call was to report about a land deal. Another was about a husband who had been accused of beating his wife.[41] Imagine having to address such issues long distance much less when you are asleep! As the King, she has to get to the root of the matter. Without determining the root cause, the mentor could administer the wrong kind of discipline. In turn, this could wound the protégé in such a way that causes the relationship to regress. When in a leadership capacity, you are serving others. When serving others, you have to be diligent in your interactions with them, to include discipline.

---

[40] Paul Schwartzman, "Peggielene Bartels: Secretary by Day, King of Otuam, Ghana, by Night," *The Washington Post,* September 16, 2009, http://www.washingtonpost.com/wp-dyn/content/article/2009/09/15/AR2009091503393.html

[41] Ibid

Correction takes patience. A good mentor will be slow to respond. Proverbs 14:29[42] declares, "A patient person shows great understanding, but a quick-tempered one promotes foolishness." Emotional responses often lead to negative repercussions. This is why it is important to pray and let the Holy Spirit be a guide. Nehemiah did not respond immediately when he heard the complaints of the people in Nehemiah 5. Legitimately, the poor Jews had an argument against the wealthy Jews who were in violation of the Mosaic Law. Jews were never supposed to charge interest to their own poor; however, the wealthy Jews were lending money to poor Jews and charging them interest and collateral. Nehemiah was visibly angry at the news, but he did not respond out of that anger. Instead, according to Nehemiah 5:7a[43], he "seriously considered the matter."

Christian mentors must be quick to hear, slow to speak, and slow to anger as James 1:19 declares. This is how Christian mentors properly assess the situation and gain understanding. When there is a proper understanding,

---

[42] Holman Christian Standard Bible, HCSB
[43] Holman Christian Standard Bible, HCSB

guidance from The Lord can be sought on how to proceed and better serve the protégé, to include respecting values.

Values

Values are those realities people believe in at the deepest level, so much so that they dictate people's decisions and their leadership. Values become a part of a person's identity. Ulrich Wickert says, "Values can neither be stolen nor transferred nor bought on credit. A purpose in life and obligations to the community cannot be simply prescribed."[44] People have to want to establish a set of values. It cannot be forced or dictated. Otherwise, people will establish a false sense of identity. Often the challenge with establishing Christian values causes people to question which Jesus they are following. Do Christians have a clear image of Christ?

Prior to becoming a Christian, a person's values were shaped by whatever community or culture they grew up in. Parents helped to develop a sense of right and wrong, good and bad. Values like integrity, trust, and

---

[44] Ulrich Wickert, *About The Loss of Values, An Essay* (Hamburg, Germany), 1994

excellence were developed. Christians learn values like submission and humility from Christ in Matthew 3:13-17.

> Then Jesus came from Galilee to John at the Jordan to be baptized by him. And John *tried to* prevent Him, saying, "I need to be baptized by You, and are You coming to me?" But Jesus answered and said to him, "Permit *it to be so* now, for thus it is fitting for us to fulfill all righteousness." Then he allowed Him. When He had been baptized, Jesus came up immediately from the water; and behold, the heavens were opened to Him, and He saw the Spirit of God descending like a dove and alighting upon Him. And suddenly a voice *came* from heaven, saying, "This is My beloved Son, in whom I am well pleased."[45]

When I speak of community and how it influences people's ability to establish values themselves, it is necessary to acknowledge the diversity this dynamic presents. God provides Christians with a set of values to live by, once they come into the saving knowledge of Him. Christians live by the premise that there is one Lord, one faith, one baptism, one God and Father of all,

Values can neither be stolen nor transferred nor bought on credit.

---
[45] Holman Christian Standard Bible, HCSB

who is above all and through all and in all.[46] However, every person a Christian encounters does not share in this premise.

As Christians establish a set of values for themselves, they must consider what they are doing. As Christian leaders, their values develop as they are tested. James 1:2-3 says, "Consider it a great joy, my brothers, whenever you experience various trials, knowing that the testing of your faith produces endurance."

While Christian's values are shaped and developed by the One who called them, Christians are better able to manage their competencies in their work. As this translates through the lens of Christ, Christians imitate Him. People are windows; unmasked individuals with a purpose that becomes clearly defined as Christians communicate more with Him. Consider 2 Corinthians 2:18: "And we all, with unveiled faces, beholding the glory of the Lord as within a mirror are being transformed into the same image from glory to glory, just as by the Spirit of the Lord."

Christians can learn valuable lessons from the Word about how values influence the Kingdom of God.

---

[46] Ephesians 4:5

Examining the life of the Apostle Paul, we learn how values can shift drastically. Saul was a persecutor of the Church; yet, one encounter changed his perspective and he became a great leader in the Kingdom of God. Much of what is learned about Kingdom values is learned from the writings of the Apostle Paul.

Christians have a responsibility to measure their personal values against the Word of God, so they can better fulfill their life's purpose. Christians are a community of believers, seeking to transcend the communities around them. Christians transcend themselves in every act of questioning and thinking, by which they demonstrate themselves to be both part of the natural world and yet simultaneously oriented toward the horizon of God, the infinite horizon of hope and love. Christian leaders exhibit the values of love and equality when they empower others. Christian leaders must value others, individually and within organizations, and seek to enhance their personal development and professional contributions to the community. To do this, Christian leaders must live the Word and lead by example.

Lead by Example

Christians must remember they operate among a mixed multitude of people; therefore, the way Christians interact with others must reflect a consistent Christian nature. This can be a challenge.

> "The Christian lives simultaneously as a Christian toward everyone, personally suffering all things in the world, and as a secular person, maintaining, using, and performing all the functions required by the law of his territory or city, by civil law and by domestic law."[47]

Christian mentors must display a *consistent* character among their protégés, especially concerning balancing their Christian walk with the secular world.

Christian leaders must be a living example of God's principles for themselves as well as for their protégés. Christians must examine their own belief systems before they can establish sound leadership practices for others. For example, a Christian leader may rely on qualities such as integrity, honesty, generosity, forgiveness, tolerance, wisdom, and compassion.[48] In order to reflect these

---

[47] Jeffrey P. Greenman, Timothy Larsen, and Stephen R. Spencer, *The Sermon on the Mount Through the Centuries* (Grand Rapids, MI: Brazos Press), 2007.

characteristics, Christians must be able to provide practical application in their day-to-day activities. An example of how Christian leaders are to conform their lifestyle to what they are teaching can be found in 1 Timothy 4:12:[49] "Let no one despise your youth; instead, you should be an example to the believers in speech, in conduct, in love, in faith, in purity."

Followers gravitate towards leaders who demonstrate traits they value.[50] When followers recognize their leaders truly follow the beliefs they have established for themselves, then they are more likely to become the same. In examining the relationship between Paul and Timothy, "the likeness he bore to him was in respect to his faith, as in human births there is a likeness in respect of substance."[51] It is important for leaders to be an example

---

[48] Rachid Zeffane (2010), "Towards a Two-Factory Theory of Interpersonal Trust: A Focus on Trust in Leadership," *International Journal of Commerce and Management* 20, no. 3, 2010: 248, doi: 10.1108/10569211011076938.

[49] Holman Christian Standard Bible, HCSB

[50] Eric Chong and Helene Wolf, "Factors Influencing Followers' Perception of Organizational Leaders," *Leadership and Organization Development Journal* 31, no. 5, 2010: 402-419, doi: 10.1108/01437731011056434.

[51] Philip Schaff, *The Homilies of St. John Chrysostom on Timothy, Titus, and Philemon Nicene and Post-Nicene Fathers Vol. 8* (Grand Rapids,

that empowers others and shows their dedication. Dr. Martin Luther King, Jr. was such a leader.

> The leader is a team builder who empowers individuals in the organization and passionately "lives the vision" thereby serving as a mentor and example for those whose efforts are necessary to make the vision a reality. An outstanding example was Martin Luther King, who lived the vision ("I have a dream") and provided a model for everyone in the civil rights movement.[52]

Mentors set the tone for the relationship with their protégé. In a Christian mentoring relationship, the relationship should be an educational cycle that has an infinite capacity surrounded by Jesus as depicted in the picture below. This is what Chris Argyris calls double-loop learning: learning to change underlying values or assumptions. When leaders seize the opportunity to teach others what they know, those leaders in turn develop other leaders. Thus, the cycle of learning continues.

Followers gravitate towards leaders who demonstrate traits they value.

MI: Christian Classics Ethereal Library), n.d.
   [52] Burt Nanus, *Visionary Leadership* (San Francisco, CA: Jossey-Bass), 1992: 14.

Diagram I.

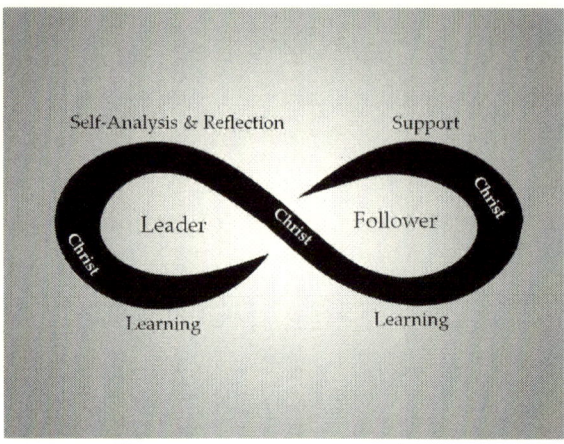

It is critical for leaders to understand that they are always mentoring others, even when they are not fully aware others are watching them as a means of mentoring.[53] Therefore, the actions and character traits leaders possess must align with their beliefs. Additionally, leaders must be cognizant of the decisions they make within their respective organizations as they develop other leaders – even in succession planning. Here is an example of how a leader's values can affect an organization.

ShoreBank was a community development bank founded in 1973 and headquartered in Chicago, Illinois. In 2008, a study was conducted regarding ShoreBank's

---

[53] Refer to the section on informal mentoring.

leadership values and approaches. The leaders wanted to know if their core beliefs, attitudes, values, and behaviors were being instilled in the next generation of leaders in the organization and in other community-development banking institutions. The study revealed that 50% of the leaders noted early influences that had a substantial impact on their values and career decisions. This, in turn, had implications for the selection and retention of leaders.[54] Unfortunately, there existed a disparity between blacks and whites. This conflicted with ShoreBank's core value on diversity.

ShoreBank realized the dysfunction within their organization. Many of the leaders they had employed had conflicting values instilled in them from leaders who mentored them. After 37 years, the Illinois Department of Financial and Professional Regulation closed ShoreBank, and the Federal Deposit Insurance Corporation (FDIC) was named receiver.[55] Leaders must be aware that what they

---

[54] Jay O. Colker, *A Grounded Theory Approach to Developing a Theory of Leadership Through a Case Study of ShoreBank,* (Unpublished doctoral dissertation, University of Phoenix, 2008)

[55] "Failed Bank Information: ShoreBank," *FDIC*, May 16, 2013, http://www.fdic.gov/bank/individual/failed/shorebank.html

impart to others has a lasting impact on who those people become as well as what happens to their organizations. Leaders establish a standard of conduct and those who follow, in turn, prescribe to it. Timothy and Titus modeled their leadership style after the Apostle Paul, who modeled himself after Christ. Christian leaders should be doing the same – modeling themselves after Christ.

Leadership development must be a key concept mentors keep in mind as they are mentoring others. People attribute behavior to stated values. So if you are saying one thing and doing another, you are the epitome of what Ralph Waldo Emerson said: "What you are speaks so loudly, I cannot hear what you say." Protégés (as well as others) study mentors. They study the mentor's actions more than the mentor's words. More importantly, as they study mentors, they align the mentor's actions with the mentor's words, especially within organizations.

There is a rich body of literature that treats leadership development as an increasingly critical and strategic imperative for organizations and argues organizations that wish to survive and succeed in today's turbulent and highly competitive business environment need to develop leadership at all levels.[56] This means the leader must interact and connect with followers everywhere. Most leaders fail to recognize and understand the capacity and breadth of their leadership; many times, leaders are mentoring more than those in their immediate sphere of influence. So, in order to "reach the masses," mentors must be willing to mingle with their protégés. Protégés need to see their mentors are interested in them and their ideas. The reason Timothy and Titus served with Paul and sought guidance from him was because they witnessed his capacity to reach others often by the way he treated them. He lived what he preached.

Matt Evans believes, "To become a leader, you must become yourself and become the maker of your destiny, thus enabling you to become the maker of a destiny for others."[57] John Borshoff is the founder, managing director and CEO of Paladin Energy. When asked what key lessons

---

[56]Afroditi Dalakoura, "Differentiating Leader and Leadership development: A Collective Framework for Leadership Development," *Journal of Management Development* 29, no. 5, 2010: 433, doi: 10.1108/02621711011039204.

[57] Matt H. Evans. "Course 18: Leadership," July 16, 2012, www.exinfm.com/training/pdfiles/course18.pdf

about entrepreneurship and successful growth strategies he had taken from company experience, he said,

> Be willing to stand alone in your beliefs. I felt I had the ability to inspire others to join me on a journey that would be exciting and challenging, knowing that if we got things right there would be a material reward following personal achievement and satisfaction.[58]

His initial take focused on what he believed and how he treated others. This is the approach leaders must take when developing themselves and others. The Apostle Paul stressed the importance of serving others. When he wrote to Titus, he urged, "The fruits of God's mercy must be seen in good conduct, otherwise the Christian profession will become a reproach."[59]

Provide Instruction

Mentors are developing other leaders by transferring to their protégés their own experience and knowledge; providing a focus for common goals and actions and setting

---

[58]George Foster, Antonio Davila, Martin Haemmig, Xiaobin He, Ning Jia, Max von Bismark, and Kerry Wellman, "Global Entrepreneurship and the Successful Growth Strategies of Early Stage Companies," *World Economic Forum,* 2011: 325.

[59]Charles F. Pfeiffer, Howard F. Vox, and John Rea, *Wycliffe Bible Dictionary* (Peabody, MA: Hendrickson Publishers), 2003: 1720.

the strategy and decision making direction for them to follow; and bringing personal satisfaction to help others grow.[60] Matt Evans says,

> Leaders need to create opportunities for young adults and children to engage in the act of leadership. When they know what "right" looks like early on, so that when they are older and participate in our institutions, they will know what are the right things to do.[61]

This is the fundamental purpose for becoming a mentor. This is seen in the relationship between the Apostle Paul and Timothy.

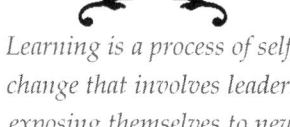

Timothy had an extraordinary opportunity to learn from Paul at an early age. Paul even admonishes Timothy not to focus on his age but the

Learning is a process of self-change that involves leaders exposing themselves to new paths they would not normally follow.

responsibility he was giving him: Paul wrote the letters (1

---

[60]Afroditi Dalakoura, "Differentiating Leader and Leadership development: A Collective Framework for Leadership Development," *Journal of Management Development* 29, no. 5, 2010: 435, doi: 10.1108/02621711011039204.

[61]Matt H. Evans, "Course 18: Leadership." July 16, 2012: 15, www.exinfm.com/training/pdfiles/course18.pdf

and 2 Timothy) to prepare Timothy to carry on the work of ministry after Paul's impending death. Timothy was going to have to rely on his memory of Paul's teaching and example as well as whatever wisdom Paul was passing along.[62]

In life, people never stop learning. Thus, the evolution of education is a continued cycle of infinite proportions. Learning is a process of self-change that involves leaders exposing themselves to new paths they would not normally follow.[63] This means increased reading and leaders allowing themselves time to think strategically. Leaders build themselves up so they can in turn build others. What does this mean? A leader must have a sense of their own ability to think and their own way of learning.

As the son of a Pharisee, the Apostle Paul was a scholar, even before his conversion. After his conversion, he learned a different way. Acts 9:15, 16 tell us that he was to

---

[62]David A. DeSilva, *An Introduction to the New Testament: Contexts, Methods, and ministry Formation* (Downers Grove, IL: InterVarsity Press), 2004: 733-734.

[63] Mette Vestergaard, "The Leader is His Own Mentor: Commentary with Mette Vestergaard," *Emerald Group Publishing Limited,* August 31, 2011, www.emeraldinsight.com.library.regent.edu/learning/management_thinking/articles/leader_mentor.htm

learn from the Lord Jesus. We find in 1 Timothy 1:12-16 that he learned through suffering. Paul constantly reflected on himself and on those things he needed to improve. He did this for the express purpose of the call and, as such, he shared what he learned with others. The same way Paul provided instruction to Timothy and Titus is the same way Christian leaders are to develop others. Provide clear instruction. Christian leaders should also not be afraid to take an inward look to make the necessary adjustments to be more effective.

Leaders must realize that followers today expect them to be more interpersonally competent in order to succeed in being truly influential as leaders. Moreover, leaders must provide feedback and instruction to bridge the gap between generations, specifically Generations X and Y (Millenials). It is important to keep in mind that Generation X (GenX) is different from Generation Y (Millenials). Both of these generations are different from the Baby Boomers. For example, Generation Y (Millenials) mistake what they do for how they perform. This creates difficulty for them and their leaders as they enter the workplace.[64] On the

---

[64] Hill Stephens, "The compassionate organization in the 21st

other hand, this same generation is more diverse and more accepting of diversity. Moreover, Millenials value relationships and learn from said perspective. Here are a few more things to remember about Millenials:

1. They tend to lean towards hands-on experiences; thus, leaders may want to develop role-playing projects centered on real issues.

2. When communicating and instructing, it is important to use practical applications. To do so, dig deep. Do not be afraid to ask the difficult questions and throw away old traditions.

3. Be realistic about how long the learning process will take. It will not occur overnight. Take advantage of their learning curve and grasp their attention at an early stage. This will yield positive results.

Mentoring in Action

We can take the same principles the Apostle Paul shared with Timothy and Titus and apply them to modern leadership development and mentoring relationships. Leadership development today is comprised of advances in globalization, technology, return on investment, and new

---

century." *Organizational Dynamics* 32, no. 4, 2003: 333. doi: 10.1016/j.orgdyn.2003.08.004

ways of thinking about the nature of leadership and leadership development. Increasingly, leadership is not defined as what the leader does but rather as a process that engenders and is the result of relationships – relationships that focus on the interactions of both leaders and collaborators instead of focusing on only the competencies of leaders.[65]

The Apostle Paul made constant reference to the time he spent with Timothy and Titus. It was the time spent together laboring in the ministry together where Timothy and Titus were able to learn from the Apostle Paul and develop their relationships with him. Their relationships developed to the point Paul referred to Titus as his brother. In 2 Corinthians 8:23, he refers to him as his partner and fellow-helper. The relationship between Paul and Timothy was so great that he referred to Timothy as his son. Timothy was his beloved friend; thus, Paul regarded him with the tenderest of affection.[66]

---

[65] Gina Hernez-Broome and Richard L. Hughes, "Leadership Development: Past, Present, and Future," *Center for Creative Leadership*, n.d.: p. 27

[66] Mark Water, *The Baker Encyclopedia of Bible People: A Comprehensive Who's Who from Aaron to Zurishaddai* (Grand Rapids, MI: Baker Books), 2006.

Barbara Kellerman makes a compelling argument regarding present day leadership.

> We need to think of leadership as a creative act – for which leaders and followers are both educated, for which leaders and followers both are prepared over a lifetime of learning . . . There are ways to educate women and men so they learn to be good, smart followers as well as good, smart leaders, and develop as large a capacity for contextual intelligence as for emotional intelligence.[67]

The challenges facing leadership has had an impact on how it has developed over the years. Much of it has to do with the culture. The history of a place will often dictate which leadership attributes are best suited; therefore, leaders have to ensure they have an array of styles available to them to be effective. Consider the violent history of Rwanda; it is understood why it is necessary to exercise wisdom. Hate and reprisal govern their method of leadership. Contrarily, South Africa has chosen a more forgiving method by forming the Truth and Amnesty Commission to offer amnesty to anyone, black or white, who would come forward and confess their crimes against humanity.[68] Paul

---

[67] Barbara Kellerman, *The End of Leadership* (New York, NY: Harper Business), 2012.
[68] Desmond Tutu, *No Future without Forgiveness* (New York, NY:

had to instruct Timothy and Titus according to their specific areas, knowing each area had a different issue.

Instead, you should be an example to the believers in speech, in conduct, in love, in faith, in purity.

From an organizational standpoint, the principle still applies. For instance, in China, a CEO is considered god. So being open-minded, trustful of others, and respectful of others is much harder to do.[69] Does this mean the Christian leader has to compromise his beliefs and live out a different set of principles in the workplace? Certainly not. In developing leaders today, Christians must be living examples and provide instruction.

1. Leaders must establish their belief systems and adhere to them in their day-to-day actions. First Timothy 4:12b provides an example of how leaders are to conform their lifestyle to what they are teaching.[70]

Image), 2000.

[69] George Foster, Antonio Davila, Martin Haemmig, Xiabin He, Ning Jia, Max von Bismark and Kerry Wellman, "Global Entrepreneurship and the Successful Growth Strategies of Early Stage Companies," *World Economic Forum*, 2011.

[70] "Instead, you should be an example to the believers in speech, in conduct, in love, in faith, in purity."

2. Leaders must also be willing to expand their thinking. The cycle of learning is continuous; therefore, leaders must immerse themselves in books, videos, and other sources of material in order to enhance their leadership abilities.

3. Lastly, leaders must be willing to share what they know with others to grow and develop future leaders.

Leaders prepare their people, develop them, challenge them, encourage them, and touch them with their vision and the passion for that vision.[71] This is exactly what the Apostle Paul did throughout his ministry. The Apostle Paul recognized that Jesus was the exemplary model of leadership. "Jesus exemplified the heart, mind and method of a servant leader, and produced extraordinary results with ordinary people."[72] With this in mind, how do you establish a leadership style?

Establishing a Leadership Style

Mentors need to know what their leadership style is. Even if their leadership style varies, depending on whom

---

[71] Bill Westfall, "Leaders Care for the Spirit," *Executive Excellence* 9, 1992

[72] Mike Hamel and Merrill Oster, "Lead Like Jesus," *Regent Business Review* 10, 2004

they are mentoring or the situation they are addressing, mentors have to identify their primary leadership style. This will help the mentor decide whether to engage in a particular mentoring relationship. A mentor's particular style of leadership may not mesh well with the person seeking their guidance. If in an organizational setting, it will be important for human resources to align the mentor's leadership style with the correct employee.

Leadership styles affect the learning ability of the protégé and speak to how the mentor will guide them in the mentoring relationship. Edmondson argues that leaders play a critical role in helping others frame and reframe knowledge and experience.[73] Individuals on the team directly observe leadership characteristics and the extent to which these characteristics help or hinder knowledge application by individuals on the team plays an influential role in the success of the project.[74] Additionally, the

---

[73] Shikhar Sarin, and Christopher McDermott, "The Effect of Team Leader Characteristics on Learning, Knowledge Application, and Performance of Cross-Functional New Product Development Teams," *Decision Sciences*, 34, 2003: 707-739, DOI: 10.111/j.1540-5414.2003.02350.x

[74] Amy Edmondson, "Framing for Learning: Lessons in Successful Technology Implementation," *California Management Review* 45, no. 2, 2003: 34-54.

mentor's leadership style will determine whether the mentor can adapt it to meet the needs of the protégé. It is also possible to combine certain leadership styles. This is combined leadership.

When thinking about combined leadership, think about a combo meal. Just about every fast food restaurant has a value meal or a combo meal. Like clockwork, when purchasing a combo meal, the attendant will ask, "Would you like to super-size that combo?" The answer will be either, "Yes" or "No." Combining the various leadership styles is possible, given certain situations. However, the mentor's core leadership style remains constant. For example, when purchasing a combo meal, the 'core' of the meal is the same. The difference is the amount of food received based on whether the person answered 'yes' or 'no' to the super-size request. When different leadership styles are combined, the core leadership style remains constant. The only difference is you get more of what you asked for.

Leadership styles affect the learning ability of the protégé and speak to how the mentor will guide them in the mentoring relationship.

A person's core leadership style is their inner world. Dr. John Townsend states, "Leading from your inner world ultimately produces better results in your leadership."[75] A person's core is the source of their values, which is the central point of their being. Here it is important to note, a person's environment as well as their cultures determine the values they adopt for themselves.[76] Personal values develop in a social context.[77] The values people learn as children shape them into the leaders they become. "Values affect leaders' moral reasoning and personal behavior."[78] Different communities / cultures establish different values. For instance, African cultures value

- a sense of community life;
- a sense of good human relations;
- a sense of sacredness of life;
- a sense of hospitality;
- a sense of the sacred and of religion;
- a sense of time;
- a sense of respect for authority and the elders; and

---

[75] John Townsend, Ph.D. *Leadership Beyond Reason: How Great Leaders Succeed By Harnessing The Power Of Their Values, Feelings, And Intuition* (Nashville, TN: Thomas Nelson), 2009.

[76] Refer to the section on values.

[77] Robert F. Russell, "The role of values in servant leadership," *Leadership and Organization Development Journal* 22, no. 2, 2001: p. 76.

[78] Ibid, p. 76

- a sense of language and proverbs.[79]

The Quichua tribe of South America believes they are one with nature. They maintain their culture based on natural powers and Shamans.[80]

> Humans transcend themselves in every act of questioning and thinking, by which they demonstrate themselves to be both part of the natural world and yet simultaneously oriented toward the mysterious horizon of being that Christians know as God, the infinite horizon of hope and love.[81]

When selecting a leadership style, the mentor will need to consider the values and cultural background of the individual or individuals they are mentoring. The mentor may, in fact, combine different leadership styles.

Diversity has a huge influence on mentoring relationships.

We can take a deeper reflection of this discussion on combined leadership and

---

[79] Unknown, "African Cultural Values," June 2, 2012, http://www.emeka.at/african_cultural_vaules.pdf
[80] El Jardin Aleman, "Quichua Indians Ecuador," June 2, 2012, http://www.eljardinaleman.com/quichua_indians.htm
[81] "Similarity, Community, Values and Human Nature: What About Those Different Folks?" *BATR*, June 2, 2012 http://www.batr.org/archives/part7.html

observe what a combination of servant leadership and charismatic leadership would look like. Eric Chong and Helene Wolf outline five attributes of servant leadership: empowerment, love, humility, trust and vision.[82] They also state, "Charismatic leaders master the use of 'impression management' to gain followers' admiration, inspire them and gain their commitment and create and sustain a heroic image."[83] If we combined servant leadership with charismatic leadership, we may end up with a leader who is able to leverage people's emotions to draw them into their sphere of influence. Once inside, they can impart into these individuals humility and love. A combination of the different leadership styles enlarges the capacity of the leader to accomplish organizational and personal goals while remaining true to the core of who they are.

A dimension mentors must consider when establishing a leadership style is diversity. In the United States, we have Title VII of the Civil Rights Act to help us

---

[82] Eric Chong, and Helene Wolf, "Factors Influencing Followers' Perception of Organizational Leaders," *Leadership and Organization Development Journal* 31, no. 5, 2010: 403, doi: 10.1108/01437731011056434

[83] Ibid, 405

govern certain inalienable rights as citizens. The Act prohibits employers from discriminating against individuals based on race, color, religion, sex, and national origin. While this is great, why can't the Act be used in everyday life? Why can't Title VII of the Civil Rights Act be viewed as a means by which people govern themselves with each other? How can we love our neighbor as we love ourselves[84] if we exhibit some form of prejudice or bias towards them?

A one size fits all style of leadership, like clothes, does not always apply. Jesus did not take this approach. He saw everyone as a unique individual. His approach was tailored to each person He encountered. This required Him to change his perspective on how He addressed each person. Mentors will have to do the same. Let us look at a few recommended leadership styles for mentoring.

Recommended Leadership Styles for Mentoring

Leadership is about people and requires a different set of skills -- influencing, explaining, listening, and

---

[84] Mark 12:31

developing, among others. To quote George Bush, "Effective leaders know that people are an asset we can enhance and develop, rather than a liability to be controlled and diminished." Once leaders come to realize their capacity to influence others, they are better equipped to choose a leadership style.

Most leaders "fall into" a particular leadership style based on their personality traits. Hill and Stephens say, "As we mature and move through the stages of our individual lives, most of us continuously add personal and professional 'selves' to a growing list of identities with implicit and explicit role responsibilities."[85] They go on to discuss the conflicts that occur within and among selves.[86]

Given the stereotypes society invokes, generational differences are lost in the shuffle. The varying degrees of generations in the workforce are a challenge for leaders today in determining "who they are" and "what their style of leadership will be." For instance, Baby Boomers are adept at holding onto previous selves as they add new

---

[85] Ronald P. Hill, and Debra L. Stephens, "The Compassionate Organization in the 21st Century," *Organizational Dynamics* 32, no. 4, 2003: pp. 331-341, doi:10.1016/j.orgdyn.2003.08.004
[86] Ibid, p. 338

ones, especially if they are associated with their (former) youthful vigor.[87] This is something to consider as we ponder this issue of leadership style.

When it comes to leadership, there is more than one method or style in existence. The style of leadership one chooses may be based on personality traits, character traits, KSA's (knowledge, skills, and abilities), and situations. One may choose to be a transformational or servant leader as their primary style of leadership, but it may not apply to all situations. There may be times when an autocratic form of leadership is applicable. This is one reason why leaders should know the different leadership theories. It increases their diversity and ability to expand their reach. Moreover, it broadens their perspective and horizons. It allows them to "reframe attitudes, beliefs, habits and cultural values in their organizations."[88]

Kurt Lewin conducted a leadership decision experiment in 1939 with some of his colleagues. They

---

[87] Ibid, p. 334

[88] Wendelin M. Kuepers, "Trans- + -form" Leader- and Followership as an Embodied, Emotional and Aesthetic Practice for Creative Transformation in Organisations," *Leadership and Organization Development Journal* 32, no. 1, 2011: 20-40, DOI: 10.1108/01437731111099265

identified three different styles of leadership, in particular around decision-making – autocratic, democratic and laissez-faire. He defined autocratic leadership as a leader who makes decisions without consulting with others. Contrarily democratic leadership involves the people in the decision-making; however, the process for the final decision may vary from the leader having the final say to them facilitating consensus in the group. A laissez-faire leader minimizes the leader's involvement and allows people to make their own decisions, although the leader may still be responsible for the outcome.

By no means are these the only styles of leadership available. Rensis Likert identified four styles of leadership – exploitive authoritative, benevolent authoritative, consultative, and participative. Exploitive authoritative leaders have a low concern for people and use such methods as threats and other fear-based methods to achieve conformance. Communication is almost entirely downwards and the psychologically distant concerns of people are ignored. Benevolent authoritative leaders add concern for people to an authoritative position. It is the equivalent of a benevolent dictatorship. In this form of leadership, the leader uses rewards to encourage appropriate performance and listens more to concerns lower down the organization, although what they hear is limited to what their subordinates think they want to hear. In consultative leadership, the leader makes an effort to listen carefully to ideas. Leaders using the participative method engage people lower down the organization. People across the organization are psychologically closer and work well together at all levels.

Effective leaders know that people are an asset we can embrace and develop, rather than a liability to be controlled and diminished.

Daniel Goleman, Richard Boyatzis and Annie McKee describe six styles of leadership in their book *Primal Leadership*. These leadership styles have different effects on the emotions of the target followers. Their six emotional leadership styles are the visionary leader, the coaching leader, the affiliative leader, the democratic leader, the pace-setting leader, and the commanding leader. In reviewing the various leadership styles, many of them (if not all of them) overlap in concept and theory.

Visionary leaders move people toward a shared vision, telling them where to go. They openly share information, empowering others. Coaching leaders connect wants to organizational goals. They help people find strengths and weaknesses and tie them to career aspirations and actions. Affiliative leaders create people connections and harmony within the organization. It focuses on emotional needs over work needs. People are most familiar with the democratic leader, who acts to value inputs and commitment via participation, listening to both the bad and the good news. Pace-setting leaders build challenge and exciting goals for people, expecting excellence and often exemplifying it themselves. They identify poor performers and demand more of them. If necessary, they will roll up their sleeves and rescue the situation themselves. Finally, commanding leaders give clear directions by his or her powerful stance, commanding and expecting full compliance. Agreement is not needed. These leaders need emotional self-control for success and can seem cold and distant.

History is full of great leaders, good and bad. Adolf Hitler was the quintessential commanding, autocratic leader. His directions were clear and he expected full compliance, whether his followers agreed with him or not. He needed emotional self-control to be successful and seemed to be a cold and distant man. *Time Magazine* wrote an article on Adolf Hitler. In the article it stated,

> The fact is that Hitler was beloved by his people – not the military, at least not in the beginning, but by the average Germans who pledged to him an affection, a tenderness and a fidelity that bordered on the irrational. It was idolatry on a national scale. One had to see the crowds who acclaimed him. And the women who were attracted to him. And the young who in his presence went into ecstasy.[89]

Unfortunately, Hitler's influence lives on in the Nazi party prevalent around the globe.

Dr. Martin Luther King, Jr. was a visionary and pace-setting leader. He moved people toward a shared vision, telling them where to go. He openly shared information, empowered others and built challenging, exciting goals for them to follow. He was not afraid to roll up his sleeves and be actively involved with the situation. His leadership was fundamental to the civil rights movement and its success in

---

[89] Elie Wiesel, "Adolf Hitler," *Time Magazine*, 1998, http://www.time.com/time/magazine/article/0,9171,988156-2,00.html

ending the legal segregation of African Americans in the South and in other parts of the United States. He is known as a transcendent symbol for his actions, speeches and leadership has spanned the millennia and continues today.

As you can see, there are a number of leadership styles and their range can be overwhelming. I have selected four particular leadership styles I feel align well with mentoring. These styles include servant leadership, situational leadership, transactional leadership, and transformational leadership. These leadership styles are in no particular order of importance.

Servant Leadership

> *The servant-leader is servant first. It begins with the natural feeling that one wants to serve. Then conscious choice brings one to aspire to lead. The best test is: do those served grow as persons; do they, while being served, become healthier, wiser, freer, more autonomous, more likely themselves to become servants?* —Robert K. Greenleaf

In looking at servant leadership, you will find it overlaps with transformational leadership. There are countless books and theories on the subject matter, all of which discuss a correlation or relationship between the two leadership styles. It is nearly impossible to talk about one without the other. While the discussions overlap concerning their virtues, there are still distinct differences between servant leadership and transformational leadership. With all of the books and research on the two leadership styles, it can be concluded that there are multiple ways to arrive at the same destination. The root of the principle remains the same; it is up to the individual leader to determine which direction or which path best suits their personality and style of leadership. Let us take some time focusing on servant leadership.

When leaders begin by viewing themselves as servants, they create stronger corporations and produce serving institutions, and they find greater personal joy in their leadership roles.

According to Greenleaf and Spears, servant leadership is a leader's desire to motivate and guide followers, offer hope, and provide a more caring experience through established quality relationships.[90] "Not until we have considered our

---

[90] Robert K. Greenleaf, and Larry C. Spears, *Servant Leadership: A Journey Into The Nature Of Legitimate Power And Greatness 25th Anniversary Edition*, (Mahwah, NJ: Paulist Press), 2002

leadership model at the level of its values, assumptions, and principles can we discern to what extent we are leading from a power or a servant base."[91] When leaders begin by viewing themselves as servants, they create stronger corporations and produce serving institutions, and they find greater personal joy in their leadership roles.[92] Hutchison says becoming an effective leader demands a transformation of one's view of leadership and authority.[93] Servant leadership is a belief that organizational goals will be achieved on a long-term basis only by first facilitating the growth, development, and general well-being of the individuals who comprise the organization.[94]

Interestingly, it can be argued that servant leadership is about empowerment since its objective is to develop the lives of its followers. Here a clear overlap

---

[91] Stacy T. Rinehart, *Upside Down: The Paradox of Servant Leadership* (Colorado Springs, CO: NavPress Publishing Group), 1998: 30.

[92] John C. Hutchison, "Servanthood: Jesus' Countercultural Call to Christian Leaders," *Bibliotheca Sacra* 166, 2009: 54.

[93] Ibid

[94] A. Gregory Stone, Robert F. Russell, and Kathleen Patterson, "Transformational versus servant leadership: A difference in leader focus," *The Leadership and Organization Development Journal* 25, no. 4, 2004: 355. doi: 10.1108/01437730410538671

between servant leadership and transformational leadership can be seen. There are other similarities as well. Both servant leadership and transformational leadership highlight the importance of trust, integrity, honesty and enlightenment. The two leadership styles place value on their followers and what their followers have to contribute to the leader/follower relationship. They both, also, focus on bringing about change – real change.

Both transformational and servant leadership embody vision, trust, honesty and integrity, modeling, service, appreciation of others, and empowerment. The servant leader does not serve with a primary focus on results, as is the transformational leader; rather the servant leader focuses on service itself.[95] Contrary to servant leadership, transformational leadership is a process of building commitment to organizational objectives and then empowering followers to accomplish those objectives.[96] In essence, transformational leadership maintains the organizational goals as its source of motivation.

---

[95] Ibid, p. 355
[96] Gary Yukl, *Leadership in Organizations* 4th *ed* (Upper Saddle River, NJ: Prentice-Hall, Inc.), 1998

The motive of the servant leader's influence is not to direct others but rather to motivate and facilitate service and stewardship by the followers themselves. It is a humble means for affecting follower behavior. Servant leaders rely upon service to establish the purposes for meaningful work and to provide needed resources.[97] Gregory Stone, Robert Russell, and Kathleen Patterson contend real servanthood is a leadership style that relies upon the influence of self-giving without self-glory.[98]

With all of the similarities, how can these two leadership styles – servant leadership and transformational leadership - differ? It has everything to do with the individual. In practice there may be a difference between transformational and servant leadership in that the function of both the organizational context in which the leaders operate and the personal values of the leaders become a factor.[99] Servant leadership takes the focus off self and

---

[97] A. Gregory Stone, Robert F. Russell, and Kathleen Patterson, "Transformational versus servant leadership: A difference in leader focus," *The Leadership and Organization Development Journal* 25, no. 4, 2004: 356. doi: 10.1108/01437730410538671
    [98] Ibid, 357
    [99] Ibid, 349-361

places it on others and the community at large. Tony May is a call center director for Verizon Wireless. He said,

> Leadership starts with an inward look at ones' self in order to set an example for those whom you are leading. A leader is about service and serving those you lead while helping them achieve their goals. They must recognize and understand they are stewards of the company.[100]

Servant leadership does not abound in "greatness" nor does it operate under the principle of "power." When followers recognize that their leaders truly follow the ideals of servant leadership, then the followers are apparently more likely to become servants themselves, which decreases customer churn and increases long-term profitability and success.[101] Larry Spears states,

> For individuals it offers a means to personal growth – spiritually, professionally, emotionally, and intellectually. ... A particular strength of servant-leadership is that it encourages everyone to actively seek opportunities to both serve and lead others, thereby setting up the potential for raising the quality of life throughout society.[102]

---

[100] Tony May, personal communication, 2012.
[101] Jim Braham, "The Spiritual Side," *Industry Week* 248, no. 3, 1999: 48-56.
[102] Larry C. Spears, "The Understanding and Practice of Servant-Leadership," *School of Leadership Studies Regent University*

Jesus, the Ultimate Servant Leader

Peter Northouse describes a servant leader as a person who first becomes a servant. This person focuses on the needs of followers and helps them to become more knowledgeable, freer, more autonomous, and more like servants themselves. He goes on to say servant leaders enrich others by their presence.[103] This is a perfect expression of the servant leadership of Jesus.

What makes Jesus the ultimate servant leader? This next statement may sound religious and a bit generic, but it is fitting. Jesus was GODLY. He was a Giver. He was Organized. Jesus was Diplomatic. He was Loving. Finally, Jesus was Yielded.

Arguably, I can say we live in a self-centered society. Turn on the television or listen to the radio and you can see or hear the ad, "It's *my* money and *I* want it now!" Even fast food is tailored to the individual. Burger King tells us we can have it our way. Go to a bookstore or look at an online book catalog, and there are thousands of *self*-help, *self*-

---

Servant Leadership Research Roundtable, 2005.
   [103] Peter Northouse, *Leadership: Theory and Practice* 4th ed (Thousand Oaks, CA: Sage Publications), 2007: 349

motivating, and personal development books. All of them are designed with one purpose in mind: to help individuals focus on themselves. While there is nothing wrong with personal development and self-improvement, there is something to be said about the individual who is more concerned about the personal development of others. Jesus was always concerned about others. This was evident in His unselfish acts of giving. He

The best servant leaders are GODLY – givers, organized, diplomatic, loving, and yielded.

looked for opportunities to be a blessing to others, whether through an encouraging word or a parable to teach them a valuable lesson. Jesus was giving even when His ministry had not officially started.

The Wedding at Cana is normally associated with Jesus' first miracle; however, it is also an example of the giving nature of Jesus. Considering the close proximity of Cana to Jesus' hometown of Jerusalem, it is likely the wedding was a relative or neighbor. In many cultures, it is customary for the hosts (in this case the bride and groom) to take care of their guests. To run out of wine would be an embarrassment and could negatively affect the family's reputation for years. It also signified the groom's inability to fulfill his role and his family lacked social connections to preserve their honor; unfortunately, this is precisely what happened.

It is likely Mary, Jesus' mother, may have been involved with the wedding preparations or had a close relationship with the bride and groom. This is how she had inside knowledge about the lack of wine. Accordingly, she petitioned Jesus to do something about it. His initial refusal did not deter her nor did she receive it as a dismissal. She simply went to His disciples and told them, "Whatever He says, do it." Mary's faith in Jesus to answer her petition was firm and evident. As His mother, she knew His heart. She knew He would not let the name of the hosts be a reproach. True to her belief, Jesus addressed the problem and some 180 gallons of wine was produced from six jars of water! When the wine was served, the guests marveled and asked the hosts why they saved the *best* wine for last!

You may be asking, "How does this reflect the giving nature of Jesus?" Jesus' initial response to His mother, Mary, in John 2:4 was, "What does this concern of yours have to do with Me, woman? My hour has not yet come." Yet, He pushed aside His desire to remain hidden – meaning He was not ready to reveal Himself to Israel at the time.

There are other accounts of Jesus' giving nature. What about the six different accounts where He fed multitudes of people? In two of the accounts (Matthew 14:13-21 and Mark 6:30-44), the disciples admonished Jesus to send the people away. But, Jesus had compassion on the people. In one account, Mark 8:1-9a, Jesus said if He were to send the people away, they would faint.

> In those days there was again a large crowd, and they had nothing to eat. He summoned the disciples and said to them, "I have compassion on the crowd, because they've already stayed with Me three days and have nothing to eat. If I send them home hungry, they will collapse on the way, and some of them have come a long distance." His disciples answered Him, "Where can anyone get enough bread here in this desolate place to fill these people?" "How many loaves do you have?" He asked them. "Seven," they said. Then He commanded the crowd to sit down on the ground. Taking the seven loaves, He gave thanks, broke the loaves, and kept on giving them to His disciples to set before the people. So they served the loaves to the crowd. They also had a few small fish, and when He had blessed them, He

said these were to be served as well. They ate and were filled. Then they collected seven large baskets of leftover pieces. About 4,000 men were there.[104]

He was more concerned about the multitude of people eating than He was with eating Himself. So, He took what He and the disciples had, blessed it, and gave it to the people to eat. On each account, there was more than enough for everyone.

There are other accounts where Jesus set aside His personal needs to meet the needs of others. He took the focus from Himself and placed it on the people around Him. More often, it was His compassion for the people that compelled Him to move. This is what Mary tapped into when she petitioned Him to address the wine situation at Cana. His ultimate act of giving was His persecution, death upon the Cross, burial, and Resurrection. In Luke 23:34, Jesus was even concerned about His persecutors.[105] He pleaded with God to have mercy on them! Perhaps this is what the Apostle Paul alluded to in Philippians 2:3-5 where he said, "Don't be selfish; don't try to impress others. Be

---

[104] Holman Christian Standard Bible, HCSB
[105] Then Jesus said, "Father, forgive them, because they do not know what they are doing.

humble, thinking of others as better than yourselves. Don't look out only for your own interests, but take an interest in others, too."[106] You must have the same attitude that Christ Jesus had.

Not only was Jesus giving, He was organized. You may wondering what I mean by "organized." When a person is organized, they have their affairs in order. They have a system in place for how things should be done. A synonym for organized is "orderly." So another way to put it is Jesus was orderly.

One of the fundamental things about organization is the way it reveals purpose. During Creation, God had a purpose in mind for everything. If we examine the animals, we see there is a purpose for them – from predatory to non-predatory. Consider the following from the *Lion King*:[107]

> *Mufasa to Simba*: Everything you see exists together in a delicate balance. As king, you need to understand that balance and respect all the creatures, from the crawling ant to the leaping antelope. *Simba to Mufasa*: But dad, don't we eat the antelope? *Mufasa to Simba*: Yes, Simba, but let me

---

[106] New Living Translation, NLT
[107] *The Lion King*, Directed by Rob Minkoff and Roger Allers, (1994; Walt Disney Pictures), Film.

explain. When we die, our bodies become the grass, and the antelope eat the grass. And so we are all connected in the great Circle of Life.

While this is a work of fiction, there is some truth in it. When animals die in their natural habitation, particularly in Rainforest regions or Sub-Saharan areas, their bodies become a natural fertilizer. This produces plant life. Herbivorous animals eat the plants, and carnivorous animals eat the herbivorous animals. What does this have to do with Jesus being organized? I am merely showing you how important organization is to anything you do.

Since organization reveals purpose, people should make sure they understand the purpose behind what they are doing. Did Jesus randomly do things or was there a pattern of behavior He followed? One thing that was clear about how Jesus organized Himself was His pattern for small groups. His first order of business was to establish a small group, i.e. His disciples. While it is true there were more than 12 disciples who sought to follow Jesus, *He* designated 12. Jesus was interested in an *interpersonal* relationship with these 12. Yet, out of that 12, there were three who were closest to Him. He met with His disciples as well as other small groups in people's homes. In Matthew 26:6, we see Jesus spending time with the 12 in the home of Simon. Even after ministering to large crowds, Jesus often retreated with His small group.

> Jesus departed with His disciples to the sea, and a large crowd followed from Galilee, Judea, Jerusalem, Idumea, beyond the Jordan, and around Tyre and Sidon. The large crowd came to Him because they heard about everything He was doing. Then He told His disciples to have a small boat ready for Him, so the crowd would not crush Him.[108]

Meeting with the 12 was Jesus' opportunity to develop and equip the disciples as leaders. He was purposeful. He was intentional. He was organized. Jesus was diplomatic!

Diplomatic? What does diplomacy have to do with anything? Contrary to popular belief, life is *not* like Burger King. People cannot have it their way. There will be times when it will be essential to exercise a great deal of diplomacy and come to some kind of common resolution for the greater good of the whole. A leader has to be skilled in dealing with people in a sensitive yet effective way. Consider Jesus' response regarding hospitality in His day.

---

[108] Mark 3:7-9, Holman Christian Standard Bible (HCSB)

Nolan argues, "With Jesus, honour and shame are deliberately confused."[109] Jewish tradition was specific about the table and who / what was allowed. Gentile food was considered unclean; yet, Jesus chose to sit with sinners and eat at the table with them. The position of the Pharisees was to uphold the law. Jesus was clear that he did not come to change the law but fulfill it. The Pharisees were looking at the law through a more traditional lens. Jesus was more radical with it. For Jesus, it was not about the food or tradition. It was about transforming people. Nathan Mitchell writes:

> It wasn't simply that Jesus ate with objectionable persons – but that he ate with anyone, indiscriminately ... The table companionship practiced by Jesus thus recreated the world, redrew all of society's maps and flow charts. Instead of symbolizing social rank and order, it blurred the distinctions between hosts and guests, need and plenty. Instead of reinforcing rules of etiquette, it subverted them, making the last first and first last.[110]

---

[109] Albert Nolan, *Jesus Before Christianity Revised Edition* (Maryknoll, NY: Orbix), 1992: 29

[110] Nathan Mitchell, "Eucharist as a Sacrament of Initiation," *Liturgy Training Publications* 90, 1990: Forum essay 2.

In another account, Jesus upset the establishment again. This time it was His account of how to address paying local taxes. In Mark 12, the Pharisees and Herodians asked Jesus if it was lawful for them to pay taxes to Caesar. Jesus knew the question was obligatory and was an attempt for them to accuse Him of something. In that time, an inscription on money was the equivalent to a form of divinity and worship. Wycliffe's Bible Dictionary explains,

> The coin therefore represented to the Jews both the hated power of the Roman government and the blasphemous imperial cult which deified the earthly ruler and demanded worship of him. Yet Jesus skillfully avoided condemning the tribute taxation.[111]

Likewise, according to the Holman Christian Standard Study Bible, Jesus supported the legitimacy of human government. The question raised to Jesus was about giving and not worship, so His response was a lesson about ownership. He is saying, "Give back to Caesar what already belongs to him."

While it may be difficult to understand how this applies to modern times, it is not that difficult to imagine.

---

[111] Charles F. Pfeiffer, Howard F. Vox, and John Rea, *Wycliffe Bible Dictionary* (Peabody, MA: Hendrickson Publishers), 2003: 1800.

Consider the Office of the President of the United States of America. The individual elected to this Office has the responsibility to enforce government and enact laws for the population as a whole and not a select group of individuals. While it may be "easy" or appear as if this role is cut and dry, it is not. This individual has to consider every possible angle: ethnicities, age groups, and sexual orientation to name a few. While the general population may not agree with the decisions, it does not negate the fact that this person is charged to govern a mass group of people.

> In exercising diplomacy, there is a constant tug of war, a game of push and shove . . . The channels are always public, and the publicity of the message guarantees that the receiving individual will react in some way, since even his non-action is publicly interpreted as a response.[112]

Consider a local church for a moment. There is a Senior Pastor who is responsible for the membership at large. While members of the local church may not agree with the Pastor allowing, for instance, homosexuals to attend the

---

[112] Vernon K. Robbins, *Exploring the Texture of Texts: A Guide to Socio-Rhetorical Interpretation* (Harrisburg, PA: Trinity Press International), 1996.

worship service, is this individual not charged to love everyone as Christ loved us?

Some decisions are controversial, at best; however, the best leaders are those who can rise to the occasion and make those decisions by looking beyond the obvious and seeing the potential outcome in the future. Diplomacy is not about approval of the masses, because realistically you will not please everyone. Sometimes it involves radical action and radical decision-making, thinking beyond the "norm" and challenging traditions. Jesus was considered radical. His diplomacy broke societal barriers and bridged the gap between the afflicted and everyone else. He brought a new visual to the community where *everyone* was accepted!

Diplomacy is not about approval of the masses, because realistically you will not please everyone. Sometimes it involves radical action and radical decision-making, thinking beyond the "norm" and challenging traditions.

What would cause Jesus to exercise diplomacy in the manner in which He did? LOVE. He responded out of His unconditional love for humanity. The Bible declares in

Proverbs 10:12b that love covers a multitude of sins. In the Hebrew, the word for cover is *kasha* (kaw-saw'). The idea behind this text is more about forgiveness. Think of it in terms of parental relationships. Regardless of how often or how bad a child offends, misbehaves, or emotionally wounds their parents, the love of that parent will cover or conceal what the child has done. When a person chooses to exercise this kind of love, what they are saying is no matter what the other person does, they will not dig up or rehash what the other person has done in the past. It is buried, gone, and forgotten. The person is making a decision to move forward. When Jesus was being persecuted and crucified, He did so in humility and love. He did not argue, and He was not bitter. His act of unconditional love was sacrifice.

Jesus was a yielded vessel. This may sound like a cliché, but it is true. A significant point in Scripture is Jesus' experience in the Garden of Gethsemane. Here, we see Jesus earnestly praying twice to God the Father to relieve Him of the impending crucifixion. We see Jesus' humanity exposed; yet, even in this, He humbled Himself in submission to God the Father's ultimate plan for His life.

Then Jesus came with them to a place called Gethsemane, and He told the disciples, "Sit here while I go over there and pray." Taking along Peter and the two sons of Zebedee, He began to be sorrowful and deeply distressed. Then He said to them, "My soul is swallowed up in sorrow – to the point of death. Remain here and stay awake with Me." Going a little farther, He fell facedown and prayed, "My Father! If it is possible, let this cup pass from Me. Yet not as I will, but as You will."[113]

As He yielded, He did it in humility (see Philippians 2:7-8).[114] Throughout His earthly ministry, Jesus said, "The Son can do nothing of Himself." A constant theme throughout the book of John is Jesus' admission that His life is not His own and everything He does comes from God the Father. Secondly, nothing Jesus did was out of selfish gain. The motives of His heart were pure. He denied Himself repeatedly for the cause of others. He honored the lives of other people. How so? He did not elevate one above another; rather, He saw people as equals. He corrected the disciples when they argued about who among them was

---

[113] Matthew 26: 36-39, Holman Christian Standard Bible (HCSB)
[114] Instead He emptied Himself by assuming the form of a slave, taking on the likeness of men. And when He had come as a man in His external form, He humbled Himself by becoming obedient to the point of death – even to death on a cross.

the greatest (see Luke 9:46 and Mark 9:34). This was one of the issues the Pharisees and Herodians had with Him.

As you lead others, you will have Pharisees and Herodians who will challenge you. They will challenge your thoughts, ideals, and even your principles. They will test you on every possible hand, all for the sake of preserving their traditions and what (in their minds) is the appropriate assessment of how things should be done. In humility and love, you must respond accordingly. Yielding does not mean go with the flow of what everyone is doing. Christian leaders must yield to the Spirit of God as well as God the Father's will for their lives. When leading and mentoring others, Christians must be obedient to Him. This requires a close relationship born out of fellowship and constant communication. This is, after all, how Jesus did it.

Christian leaders must be servant leaders like Jesus: GODLY. They must be willing to give unselfishly of themselves. They must be organized and able to exercise diplomacy. They must do all things in love. Finally, they must yield themselves to God's plans.

Situational Leadership

Situational leadership is not difficult to understand. If you are asking yourself, "Is this what I think it is?" you are possibly correct! As the name implies, situational leadership is about responding to situations. Yes, it is that simple! With situational leadership, it is important to note that a "one size fits all" or a cookie-cutter approach will not work. Why? Every situation requires a different response. A person would not attempt to fit a square object into a round hole. Likewise, it is not likely a person will approach a lion the same way they would approach a house cat. Are they a similar species? Yes, but a lion is more ferocious than a house cat. In like manner, the leader must be able to adapt and adjust their style to fit the situation. Northouse believes leaders cannot lead using a single style; they must be willing to change their style to meet the requirements of the situation.[115] Overall, the leader must be flexible.

More often than not, a one-size fits all approach will not work.

---

[115] Peter J. Northouse, *Leadership: Theory and Practice 4th Edition* (Thousand Oaks, CA: Sage Publications), 2007: 97

Northouse shares with us four distinct classifications of situational leadership that include both directive (task) behaviors and supportive (relationship) behaviors. Directive behaviors help group members accomplish goals by giving directions, establishing goals and methods of evaluation, setting time lines, defining roles, and showing how the goals are to be achieved.[116] They also clarify, often with one-way communication, what is to be done, how it is to be done, and who is responsible for doing it.[117] Contrastingly, supportive behaviors help group members feel comfortable about themselves, their coworkers, and the situation.[118] It involves two-way communication and responses that show social and emotional support to others.[119] I call this the "feel good" behavior.

Now that we understand directive and supportive behaviors, we need to know more about the four classifications of situational leadership. The four classifications of situational leadership are directive, coaching, supporting, and delegating. Northouse provides

---

[116] Ibid, 93
[117] Ibid, 93
[118] Ibid, 93
[119] Ibid, 93

us with a clear understanding of each of these classifications.[120]

1. The directing style involves a high directive-low supportive behavior pattern. The leader focuses communication on goal achievement and spends a smaller amount of time using supportive behaviors.

2. The coaching style is a high-directive-high supportive pattern of behavior. Here, the leader focuses on communication on both achieving goals and meeting the follower's socioemotional needs.

3. In the supporting approach, the leader takes a high supportive-low directive style. The leader does not focus exclusively on goals but uses supportive behaviors that bring out the follower's skills around a specific task to be accomplished.

4. Delegating has a low supportive-low directive style. The leader offers less task input and social support, facilitating the follower's confidence and motivation in reference to the specific task. The leader's involvement in planning, control of details, and goal clarification decreases.

In situational leadership, it appears as if the leader actually follows the follower. This may sound strange, but the leader's response is directly proportionate to the

---

[120] Ibid, 93-94

follower's needs. The response determines the style of approach the leader is using. Think of it like this: In a monarchy, there is a ruler. The ruler has a designated place and / or group of people they (the ruler) leads. For instance, we can look at the ancient Egyptian dynasties. The Egyptian dynasties first began to decline around 2200 BC. This period was marked by political and social upheaval, confusion, and uncertainty.[121] By 1090 BC, the Egyptian dynasty was no more. On multiple occasions, various foreign countries dominated Egypt. Eventually, Egypt became a Roman province in 31 BC.[122] The situation in Egypt changed from a booming place of architectural innovation and, due to the rich soil from the Nile River, agricultural prosperity. Unfortunately, from one dynasty to the next, the kings were unable to adapt.

Most notably, we can point to the Egyptian Pharaoh who failed to address the situation with Moses in the book of Exodus. On multiple occasions, the Pharaoh faced the decision to free the enslaved Israelites and on multiple

---

[115] Charles F. Pfeiffer, Howard F. Vox, and John Rea, *Wycliffe Bible Dictionary* (Peabody, MA: Hendrickson Publishers), 2003: 502.
[122] Ibid, 503

occasions, he declined. The Bible declares Pharaoh's heart grew harder. Pharaoh looked at the situation from his perspective rather than the people's perspective. Rather than follow the lead of the people and addressing their needs and concerns, he opted to ignore them and focus on what he had planned. He was determined to keep directing. In situational leadership, the leader must be willing to look at the entire situation and come up with a solution to address the needs of the *whole* situation. Here are two things leaders must consider when applying situational leadership:[123]

1. Followers are at a high development level if they are *interested* and *confident* in their work and they know how to do a specific task.
2. Followers are at a low development level if they have little skill for a specific task but feel as if they have the motivation or confidence to get the job done.

Pharaoh's problem was that he was leaning towards a transactional style of leadership, but he still did not get it right. In his mind, it was in the best interest of the Israelites to do what he wanted them to do. An even bigger problem

---

[123] Peter J. Northouse, *Leadership: Theory and Practice 4th Edition* (Thousand Oaks, CA: Sage Publication), 2007: 94

was that Pharaoh really did not understand the true meaning of transactional leadership. In the next section, we will explore this further.

Transactional Leadership

Transactional leadership tends to be a bit selfish from the perspective of the leader in that the leader does not focus on the follower's personal development. The follower's needs are not a focal point. In transactional leadership, the leader exchanges things of value with their followers to advance their own and their follower's agendas.[124] This is what Pharaoh missed! He was not concerned with the Israelite's agenda.

In transactional leadership, there is usually a reward or punishment involved. In the case of Pharaoh and the Israelites, Pharaoh bent towards the punishment end of the spectrum. Consider the relationship between a teacher and a student. The teacher may negotiate with the student an extended deadline to submit a project without penalty in order to keep the student from failing. The reward is the

---

[124] Peter J. Northouse, *Leadership: Theory and Practice 4th Edition* (Thousand Oaks, CA: Sage Publication), 2007: 185

student's opportunity to pass the class. The punishment, if you will, is a failing grade if the student does not submit the project by the agreed upon deadline. This is called a contingency reward. The reward received is based upon the effort the follower contributes to the relationship. In the case of Pharaoh and the Israelites, it is likely the Israelites could have continued to perform up to and above Pharaoh's demands and he still would not have relented and rewarded them with what *they* wanted. To sum up transactional leadership, I like what Dr. David J. Gyertson argues,

> As faith-oriented leaders, we are called to a challenging and difficult responsibility to model leadership that is both relational and transactional in its formulations and applications. To succeed in this calling, we must embrace a whole person model of leadership learning, living and serving which, at its core, is a process of spiritual awakening and formation. At the very heart of this calling is a commitment to whole person development designed to produce spiritually formed leaders able to change their world through stretched minds, cradled hearts and reformed hands known for their noble, effective and sacrificial service.[125]

---

[125] David Gyertson, Ph.D., "A Devoted Christian's View on Development of Spiritually Formed Leadership," *International Journal of*

Transformational Leadership

In 1984, the world was introduced to a cartoon comic by the name of *Transformers*. This cartoon was the brainchild of Hasbro and the Japanese toy company Takara. The cartoon comic centered around two opposing robot forces, the Autobots and the Decepticons. These robots had the ability to transform after years of evolution and during the 2nd Cybertronian War. After years of evolution, much like the *Transformers*, mankind is still trying to transform themselves. Men are trying to be better fathers, husbands, brothers, and sons. Women are trying to be better mothers, wives, sisters, and daughters. Still there are those who are trying to transform themselves into better leaders.

Warren Bennis and Burt Nanus created a leadership model for transformational leaders after studying ninety leaders and managers.[126] They stated leaders were endowed with the following traits: logical thinking, persistence, empowerment, and self-control.

Spiritual Leadership, 2007.

[126] Warren Bennis, and Burt Nanus, *Leaders: Strategies for Taking Charge* (New York: Collins Business), 2007.

"Transformational leaders make followers into self-empowered leaders and into change agents."[127]

According to Bennis and Nanus, there are four I's of transformational leadership. The first is idealized influence. This depicts the leader as a role model. The second is inspirational motivation. The leader creates an atmosphere prime for team spirit, motivation, meaning and challenge.

Transformational leaders make followers into self-empowered leaders and into change agents.

The third is intellectual stimulation. The leader is creative and innovative. Finally, transformational leadership is individual consideration. The leader is a mentor. Again, we can point to Jesus as a transformational leader.

Bob Briner and Ray Pritchard describe Jesus' leadership like this: "Jesus had no paid staff and no marketing department, yet He inspired others to carry His message around the world. Jesus was the greatest, most inspiring leader in history."[128] Jesus knew how to command

---

[127] Ibid

[128] Bob Briner, and Ray Pritchard, *The Leadership Lessons of Jesus: A Timeless Model for Today's Leaders* (Nashville, TN: Broadman and Holman Publishers), 1997

an audience, because He recognized and understood to whom He was speaking. This is why He tailored His parables towards his audience, whether it was an individual, a crowd, or the disciples.[129] In order to clearly and effectively express His vision and values, Jesus had to tailor his conversation towards the people.

To be a transformational leader using Bennis' and Nanus' model of leadership required Jesus to be a role model. There was no greater role model in human history than The Lord. He led by example as a servant leader. Servant leader? But I thought we were talking about transformational leadership. Yes, we are; however, earlier I discussed how servant leadership and transformational leadership overlapped and how difficult it was to discuss one without the other. Due to His ability to motivate others, Jesus was able to be a change agent, and thus create change agents out of his disciples.

In an interview with Oster and Hamel in 2004, Ken Blanchard said that Jesus exemplified the heart, mind and

---

[129] Steven K. Scott, *The Greatest Man Who Ever Lived: Secrets For Unparalleled Success And Unshakable Happiness From The Life Of Jesus* (New York: Doubleday Publishing Group), 2009.

methods of a servant leader and produced extraordinary results with ordinary people. Jesus was, also, a humble leader. He thought less of himself and more of others.[130] Mr. Blanchard continued to say that humility and vision are not mutually exclusive. The first is the fulcrum while the latter is the lever that moves people.

Jesus was an inspiring motivator. He moved crowds of witnesses throughout his earthly ministry. People would come from miles around to hear and see Jesus. Word of His ministry and teaching spread like wildfire throughout the land. His ability to teach the Word (Torah) was compelling and unparalleled (see Mark 1:22). "No one could listen to Jesus without sensing in him a tremendous earnestness about life and the way it should be lived."[131]

Deborah Jenks says that Jesus' creative essence was in the parables.[132] He drew the hearer / reader into His parables, and then expected them to reflect on how their life

---

[130] Merrill Oster, and Mike Hamel, "Lead Like Jesus: Why Ken Blanchard's Latest Project Will Be His Most Important" *Regent Business Review,* no. 10, 2004: 4-6.

[131] Charles F. Pfeiffer, Howard F. Vox, and John Rea, *Wycliffe Bible Dictionary* (Peabody, MA: Hendrickson Publishers), 2003.

[132] Deborah F. Jenks, "Transformation: An Examination of Jesus' Creative Use of the Matthew 13 Parables and Theory U." (School of Global Leadership and Entrepreneurship, Regent University), 2008.

compared to the parable. One thing about the way Jesus instructs and guides, He provides people with a practical way of exercising God's Word. As a mentor, the transformational leader must be able to demonstrate their intention and teach others how to sustain it over the course of time.[133] Effective mentors know how to nurture the skills within others but recognizing their strengths and to discern the fit between their strengths and weaknesses and those of the mentee.[134]

Jesus knew how to set direction during the turbulent times with which He lived. As He mentored the disciples, following His Crucifixion, they were more able to translate His direction during the turbulent times when the Jewish communities were led by Pharisees, rabbis who assumed leadership of the Jewish people in the aftermath of the destruction of Jerusalem. They were pushed out of the larger communities, located in northern Galilee or Syria.[135]

---

[133] Warren Bennis, and Burt Nanus, *Leaders: Strategies for Taking Charge* (New York: Collins Business), 2007.

[134] Ibid

[135] Marilyn Mellowes, "The Gospel of Matthew: Writing for a Jewish Christian Audience, Matthew's Main Concern Is to Present Jesus as a Teacher Even Greater Than Moses." *Frontline*, 1998, http://www.pbs.org/wgbh/pages/frontline/shows/religion/story/mmmatthew.html June 18

The disciples were also able to manage, attract resources, and forge new alliances to accommodate new constituencies; thus, harnessing diversity on a global scale.[136] As their mentor, Jesus inspired a sense of optimism, enthusiasm, and commitment among their followers; the disciples became leaders of leaders.[137]

Wycliffe's Bible Dictionary expresses, "Even apart from supernatural aid the disciples could never forget the stirring scenes that they had shared with the Master."[138] What greater transformational leader than Jesus the Christ? By far the best example of leadership He portrayed was His Passion for humanity. As He endured the suffering of the Crucifixion and death on the Cross, from His lips came no execration, but instead a

Transformational leaders strive to align their own and others' interests with the good of the group, organization, and society.

---

[136] Warren Bennis, and Burt Nanus, *Leaders: Strategies for Taking Charge* (New York: Collins Business), 2007.
[137] Ibid
[138] Charles F. Pfeiffer, Howard F. Vox, and John Rea, *Wycliffe Bible Dictionary* (Peabody, MA: Hendrickson Publishers), 2003.

prayer for His tormentors.[139] Transformational leaders have the ability to understand people and generate trust.

Transformational leaders transform the personal values of followers to support the vision and goals of the organization by fostering an environment where relationships can be formed and by establishing a climate of trust in which visions can be shared.[140] Jeanine Parolini, Kathleen Patterson, and Bruce Winston believe, "Transformational leaders strive to align their own and others' interests with the good of the group, organization, and society."[141] In essence, transformational leadership is a process of building commitment to organizational objectives and then empowering followers to accomplish those objectives.[142] McGuire and Hutchings argue transformational leadership converts followers into leaders and results in the motivational and moral elevation of both

---

[139] Ibid

[140] Bernard M. Bass, *Leadership and Performance Beyond Expectations.* (New York, NY: The Free Press), 1985.

[141] Jeanine Parolini, Kathleen Patterson, and Bruce Winston, "Distinguishing between transformational and servant leadership," *Leadership and organization Development Journal* 30, no. 3, 2009: 274-291, doi: 10.1108/01437730910949544

[142] Gary Yukl, *Leadership in Organizations 4th Edition* (Upper Saddle River, NJ: Prentice-Hall, Inc.), 1998.

followers and leaders.[143] This occurs not only on a local level but also on a global scale.

With over 7 billion people on the planet, it is a strong possibility a person will encounter someone outside of their culture. As we look at servant, situational, transformational, and transactional leadership, it is important to incorporate the globalization aspect of leadership. Northouse tells us globalization has created the need for leaders to become competent in cross-cultural awareness and practice.[144] He goes on to describe five cross-cultural competencies:

1. Leaders need to understand business, political, and cultural environments worldwide;

2. They need to learn the perspectives, tastes, trends, and technologies of many other cultures;

3. They need to be able to work simultaneously with people from many cultures;

4. Leaders must be able to adapt to living and communicating in other cultures; and

---

[143] David McGuire, and Kate Hutchings, "Portrait of a transformational leader: The legacy of Dr. Martin Luther King Jr.," *Leadership and Organization Development Journal* 28, no. 2, 2007: 154-166, doi: 10.1108/01437730710726840

[144] Peter Northouse, *Leadership: Theory and practice 4th Edition* (Thousand Oaks, CA: Sage Publications), 2007: 302.

5. They need to learn to relate to people from other cultures from a position of equality rather than cultural superiority.

Additionally, Northouse says, "Ethnocentrism can be a major obstacle to effective leadership because it prevents people from fully understanding or respecting the world of others."[145] Environmental uncertainty represents an important contingency for organization structure and internal behaviors.[146] Leaders must recognize their leadership style affects the organization. According to William Pirraglia,[147]

> Leadership styles have strong effects on corporate culture because employees tend to act in ways that mirror their leaders. Staff also subconsciously wants to please supervisors and management. Over time, leaders and employees usually become "comfortable" with each other, which can cause some "culture friction" when new leaders take over. Every business, regardless of size, has a culture. It can help or hurt operations, often dependent on the strength and efficiency of leadership.

---

[145] Ibid

[146] Richard L. Daft, *Theory and Design of Organizations* 10th Edition (Singapore: Cengage Learning), 2010: 228.

[147] William Pirraglia, "The Effects of Leadership Styles on the Organization," http://smallbusiness.chron.com/effects-leadership-styles-organization-10387.html

Sometimes this means stepping away from traditional methods of leadership within the organization. A person may find by doing this they are characterized as a "revolutionary," but sometimes a person has to take the road less traveled. Christian leaders will often take the road less traveled following the example of The Lord Jesus. Jesus was a revolutionary leader who often took the road less traveled. His style of leadership took into consideration the structure of the organization He was leading. Just as Jesus aligned His leadership style with that of the Church, so too must today's leaders align their leadership style with their organization's structures in order to realize long-term, sustainable results. Irrespective of leadership style and abilities, whether as an individual or within an organization, leaders must be willing and able to adapt their style to the changes of today.

Now that we have an understanding of the mentor's role, to include recommended leadership styles, it is time to turn our attention to the protégé's role. How does one pursue choosing a mentor? What characteristics do you look for? How do you examine a candidate for mentorship?

The next chapter addresses these things and more. Let us proceed …

Choosing a Mentor

> *God did not create you to be alone. He deposited skills, knowledge, and talents in someone out there who is expected to mentor you, teach you and encourage you to go high. Go, get a mentor! ~ Israelmore Ayivor*

Up to this point, the focus has been aimed at being a mentor. However, it is important to devote some time to the protégé so the protégé can maximize their experience in the mentoring relationship. We are not here by accident. God created everyone and everything for a purpose. No one person is knowledgeable of all things. Everyone has something to contribute. For this reason, people are experts in certain fields of study. Most people are experts in things that come natural to them. They have discovered their purpose and are pursuing it. Many of them have elected to share their expertise with others in the hopes of continuing their passion and drive for the respective discipline. On the other side of this equation is the knowledge seeker. This person is striving towards greatness in the same discipline but lacks the guidance or knowledge on how to navigate through it. These individuals are the ones who need mentors, preferably those with strong leadership skills. While some experts in particular fields of study are good at what they do, they may lack the leadership skills to guide someone else. For this reason, it is important for the protégé (the knowledge seeker) to have a firm grasp of whom they are and what they hope to achieve in order to connect properly with a mentor.

Defining a Protégé

I define a protégé as someone who has agreed to submit to the authority of a mentor with the intent to learn and grow from them. A protégé must be purposeful, willing to learn, upright, and a steward of the resources and information the mentor shares with them. This is the PLUS side of being a protégé. A purposeful protégé is determined and intentional in their efforts to improve. This will require the protégé to be willing to learn. The protégé cannot be dogmatic, determined to be uncompromising in their way of thinking or doing things. An open-mind is necessary and required. Additionally, the protégé must be upright. It is unlikely the mentoring relationship will address the protégé's needs if the protégé is dishonest, immoral, or unethical. Finally, the protégé must be a steward of the resources and information the mentor shares with them. This shows the mentor the protégé is serious and dedicated to improving.

Protégé's must be coachable. The purpose of entering into a mentoring relationship is to grow and achieve certain goals. The mentor will not only tell the protégé what the protégé wants to hear but also what the protégé needs to hear. This information is for the protégé's correction and reproof. It lifts the protégé up to a level where the protégé normally would not reach on their own. The mentor is pushing the protégé to excel to levels beyond the protégé's own understanding. The mentor sees something in the protégé and has received some kind of vision or has discerned something about the protégé's character that needs developing. The protégé may see one thing, but the mentor sees something different. The protégé's perspective may be to hone in on a particular skill or talent, but the

A purposeful protégé is determined and intentional in their efforts to improve.

mentor may see another area the protégé needs to develop that will achieve the result the protégé is striving to attain.

The protégé must be willing to open themselves up to the mentor. The protégé must trust the mentor's judgment. At some point, the protégé will have to believe in the mentor. Otherwise, the likelihood of the mentoring relationship being successful is slim to none. If you as the protégé are uncomfortable with the mentor or your spirit does not connect with them, it is not a good relationship to pursue.

What are some characteristics to look for in a mentor? First, the protégé begins by identifying what their needs are. In addressing their needs, the protégé will need to examine themselves. This self-examination includes gaining a better understanding of who the protégé is (what makes them, them) and what the protégé values.

What Are Your Needs

> *"The difference between followers and leaders is that followers need leaders to help them follow what leaders themselves are following. This relationship takes the form of a shared response-ability to a shared calling. Both find each other in a true*

fellowship to create the world responsibly." ~ James Maroosis

In order to form this shared response-ability to a shared calling that Maroosis speaks of, the protégé (or follower as Maroosis says) must have a clear understanding of what their specific needs are. What do you need to work on to grow into the leader you desire to become? Do you have a problem with procrastination? Are you disorganized? Are you pessimistic? Do you lack vision? Maybe it is something altogether different. Perhaps you are detail-oriented, focused, and able to make on-the-spot decisions, but you lack innovation and creativity. It may be you have difficulty networking and meeting people. You may even have a problem with rejection. Whatever it is, as the protégé, you have to identify it.

How do you identify a need? First, understand that a need is a gap between what is and what is to be, where a person is and where they want to go, and who a person is and who they want to become. A simple way to identify needs is by completing a needs assessment, which is a systematic set of procedures used to determine needs, examine the nature and cause(s) of those needs, and to set priorities for future action.[148] A needs assessment helps a protégé to plan their course of action for selecting a mentor, because the protégé's goals are defined once they complete it.

Where do you begin with a needs assessment? One method for completing a needs assessment is to do a SWOT analysis. A SWOT analysis identifies strengths, weaknesses, opportunities, and threats. What are your current strengths? What are some things you need to improve? What are some opportunities for growth? What are some barriers to those opportunities? What are some things that threaten the success of your growth and development? It is important to identify these hindrances, so you and your mentor can develop a strategic plan to address them. To begin the SWOT analysis, create a list of words that describe you. However the SWOT analysis is approached, examine it from an internal as well as an external perspective. If you draw a blank or are not confident in your approach to the SWOT analysis, take a career and/or

---

[148] United States Department of Education, "Comprehensive needs assessment" [PDF document], 2001, http://www2.ed.gov/admins/lead/account/compneedsassessment.pdf

temperament assessment. There are many available via the Internet.

You may be wondering whether the protégé should be conducting this assessment with their chosen mentor. While the protégé should complete an in-depth assessment with their mentor, one that builds upon what the protégé has already begun, the protégé needs an assessment to help guide them initially. If the protégé is unclear on what their needs are, how will the protégé know if the person they are prospecting as a mentor can meet those needs? At this point, the SWOT analysis does not have to be in-depth. As I stated, there are many online resources available to help give you a start. Once you have an idea of what your needs are, you can compare them with where you want to go.

Another thing to keep in mind when looking for a mentor and determining your needs is gaining a full understanding of your personal learning style. There are four basic learning styles. These styles include:

- Auditory Learner – learns by listening and verbalizing; prefers to have information explained rather than reading the information themselves

- Kinesthetic Learner – learns by using all of their senses; uses "hands-on" approach to problem-solving; uses trial and error; slow decision-maker
- Read-Write Learner – prefers information to be written
- Visual Learner – learns by seeing and visualizing

Finally, protégés must be clear on what their personal values are. Again, the protégé begins by writing a list of words they feel define them. The protégé should think about situations and experiences they have had. How did they approach them? The protégé should think about feedback they have received from employers, co-workers, friends, and even relatives. What are some key words that repeatedly come to mind when they describe the protégé? Next, the protégé should think of how they want to be defined. For instance, the protégé may value honesty and integrity but want to add excellence as a core value. Make this clear in the list. I recommend dividing the list into two parts. The first part defines the protégé's current core values and the second part defines the protégé's desired core values. The same words may be on both lists.

Current Core Values	Desired Core Values
Chronically late	Always on time
Dishonest	Honest
Poor communicator	Effective communicator
Procrastinator	Complete tasks on time

Perhaps there are values the protégé currently has the protégé prefers not to have, like procrastination. Yes, procrastination is a value. Remember, our environments shape our values. If the protégé grew up in an environment where procrastination was normal and it was acceptable to be late, then procrastination and poor time management is a value. While it may be culturally acceptable, it may not be acceptable with the people with whom the protégé is interacting. For instance, remember when I talked about Edward T. Hall's discussion on the differences in how people address the issue of time? He identified polychronic cultures from monochromic cultures. Recall the example I gave about a polychronic individual being chronically late to meetings. It is not that they are rude, but it is a part of who they are and where they are from. If the protégé is a polychromic person, the protégé may want to break this particular value. Yes, it is important for others to recognize that all behavior makes sense through the eyes of the person behaving and that logic and rationale are culturally relative;[149] however, when establishing a relationship based upon a mutual response-ability, both parties must be willing to reach an understanding. This may require flexibility from both as the relationship develops. Now that we have a better understanding of what the protégé's role is in selecting a mentor, we can explore the mentoring model, PILLAR.

---

[149] Nancy J. Adler, "Communicating Across Cultural Barriers," *International Dimensions of Organizational Behavior 2nd Edition* (Boston, MA: PWS-KENT Publishing Company), 1991: 64.

PILLAR

> *There is only one secure foundation: a genuine, deep relationship with Jesus Christ, which will carry you through any and all turmoil. No matter what storms are raging all around, you'll stand firm if you stand on His love. ~ Charles Stanley*

Earlier in the introduction of this book, I stated, "If you are the mentor, it is important to remember that you serve as a cornerstone, a PILLAR, a support system for the person or people you are mentoring. You are a structural foundation to help build said individual(s)." I stand by that statement, because it is a fundamental of anything you build. A mentoring relationship is something built over time. A house is not built without first establishing a strong foundation for it to stand upon. Anything worth building must have a solid foundation. A mentoring relationship is no different. This model for mentoring parallels a parent-child relationship. In a mentoring relationship, there are stages as there are stages with a parent-child relationship. This chapter reveals the stages and they are built, one upon the next, to create a type of staircase. Picture a winding staircase. This is what I have in mind for this model. Once the relationship has been built to where it seems as if it cannot continue to grow, the mentor and the protégé find something else to build and grow. It is a winding relationship that grows infinitely as it deepens. First, let's learn a little bit of information about the history of columns. This will give us an understanding of why they are important and why each stage of the relationship must be sound before moving on to the next.

  The history of columns dates back to the Bronze Age and the time of the Egyptians. The type of column used often dictated its placement within the temple; thus, most temples actually employed more than one design. Additionally, the materials used to build these columns varied from location to location and age to age. The Egyptians used stone for their columns while the Minoans used tree trunks. According to the Encyclopedia of Ancient History, The Greek temples in the 8th to mid-7th centuries BCE at Isthmia, Ephesus and Corinth are believed to have employed wooden columns with stone bases alongside other structural elements in stone.

The column allowed for the support of ceilings without the use of solid walls, thereby increasing the space which could be spanned by a ceiling, allowing the entrance of light and offering an alternative aesthetic to building exteriors. Columns also could be incorporated within walls or be freestanding and carry sculpture to commemorate particular events or people.[150] Mark Cartwright declares, "Columns became so much a part of the aesthetic look of a building that the columns themselves began to become independent artistic elements." He cites some of the most famous freestanding columns are the Ionic Naxian Sphinx column at Delphi (560 BCE)[151] and Trajan's Column in Rome (113 CE).[152]

You may be asking, "What is so important about this?" Columns are foundations, support systems. They are the strength of the building or structure they are supporting. It is important to understand how they are made to see why they are so strong and why they were placed the way they were placed in the temples. When

---
[150] Mark Cartwright, "Column," *Encyclopedia: Ancient History,* 2012, http://www.ancient.eu.com/column/
[151] Before the Common/Current/Christian Era
[152] Common/Current/Christian Era

people make the decision to become mentors, the strength of that relationship hinges upon them and how solid they are as leaders. The mentor is the cornerstone and architect of the relationship. While it is true the protégé has (and should have) input into the nature of the relationship, the mentor establishes the direction and blueprint of that relationship.

Just as the columns of ancient times were erected from different materials, the mentoring relationship will be built with different material. The mentor will use a combination of things to help build the protégé. No two relationships are the same; each has a different, unique footprint based on the dynamics of the individuals involved. Therefore, what the mentor will use to help build one protégé may not be what the mentor uses to build another. Additionally, the mentoring relationship will take on a persona just like the columns of ancient times. Those columns became works of artistic expression and so will the mentoring relationship. The mentoring relationship will be an expression of the mentor's leadership style and abilities. The protégé is a walking expression and reflection of the mentor. Mentors need to keep this in mind as they consider engaging in a mentoring relationship. Regardless of how many people a mentor is mentoring, remember the relationship builds over time. Like the Egyptian columns of old, which were usually built up in sectional blocks, the mentoring relationship must be built one section at a time.

The model I have developed defines the different stages of the mentoring relationship. In life, we progress in stages; thus, this model mirrors some of those stages. The name of the model is called PILLAR.

PILLAR

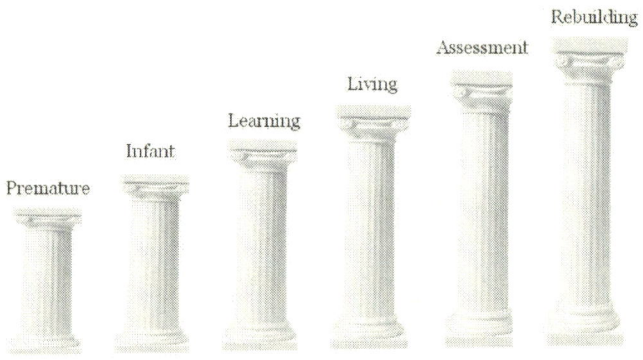

The following sections discuss each stage in detail. It is important to include possible limitations to the model, which will be discussed in a separate chapter. Keep in mind the concept of the model parallels a parent-child relationship, as indicated in the introduction of the book. Before we continue our journey, let me discuss Kathy Kram's work on mentoring and some possible limitations to the PILLAR model.

Kram's Mentoring Phases

Kathy Kram is the Richard C. Shipley Professor in Management at Boston University and is an expert in the field of mentoring. In 1983, she published an article in the Academy of Management Journal about the phases of the mentoring relationship. She said, "Adult development perspectives suggest that the primary task of early adulthood is one of *initiation*, and the primary task of middle adulthood is one of *reappraisal*."[153] In her work, she studied 18 relationships at a northeastern public utility company. Because of the study, Kram determined, although developmental relationships vary in length (average length of five years in the research sample), they generally proceed through four predictable, yet not entirely

---

[153] Kathy E. Kram, "Phases of the Mentor Relationship," *The Academy of Management Journal* 26, no. 4, 1983: 608.

distinct, phases: an initiation phase, a cultivation phase, a separation phase, and a redefinition phase.[154]

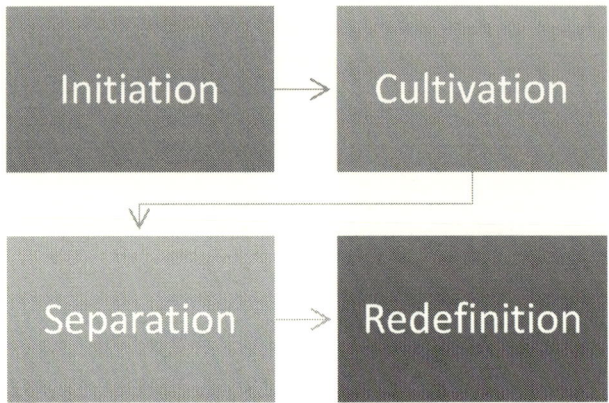

The initiation phase is the beginning of the relationship and reflects on the first 6 to 12 months of the relationship. It serves to transform "initial fantasies into concrete positive expectations."[155] From the second to the fifth year, the cultivation phase emerges. During the cultivation phase, the boundaries of the relationship have been clarified, and the uncertainty of what it might become during the initiation phase is no longer present.[156] Also during the second to fifth year, the separation phase comes into play. It is like the great equalizer of the cultivation phase: Once the individuals involved realize the

---

[154] Ibid, 614
[155] Ibid, 615
[156] Ibid, 617

relationship cannot continue in the same direction, a decision is made to move on. In the final phase, redefinition, the relationship transitions into a friendship. "Both individuals continue to have some contact on an informal basis in order to continue the mutual support created in earlier years."[157] This phase, also, reflects changes that have occurred in the people involved in the relationship. Based off the work Kram began in 1983, the author developed a mentoring model that can be used to define the evolution of the mentoring relationship. This model can be used in formal and informal mentoring relationships.

Possible Limitations to the Model

Nothing is perfect. There are limitations to everything. As human beings, our bodies have limits. As such, when our bodies reach or exceed those limits, we experience the repercussions. The PILLAR model is no different. There are limitations to it. One limitation is a possible mismatch of the mentor's leadership style with the protégé's learning curve. Another limitation is if the mentor

---

[157] Ibid, 620

has selfish motives for accepting the mentoring opportunity. What if the mentor is unqualified and proceeds with the mentoring relationship despite this fact? Unfortunately, this kind of incompatibility occurs more often than not. It points back to the mentor's selfish motives. Some people engage in mentoring relationships because it makes them feel good about themselves. While there is nothing wrong with feeling fulfilled from helping others, if the mentor's intent is to increase their popularity and to promote himself or herself, the mentor has entered the relationship for the wrong reason. As a Christian mentor, this violates the basic Biblical principle of *serving* others.

Another limitation is ambivalence and disobedience from the protégé. If ambivalence and / or disobedience from the protégé is experienced, it is likely trust has either not been established or it has been broken. In order to solidify trust, the mentor must:

> 1. Care about the protégé in a thoughtful way, but at the same time, hold them accountable for what they do.

2. Honor commitments to them – the mentor should do as they say.

3. Communicate and reach the protégé in a way that shows respect, recognizing that differences are a sign of progress.

4. Follow a set of values the protégé can identify with – integrity, courage, reliability, fairness, and a lack of selfishness.

Trust is like a thread running through everything, providing a grounding pillar for making leadership happen.[158]

Another reason for the ambivalence or disobedience is the protégé may feel as if the mentor has not addressed their needs. Examine the situation and openly discuss it. If the protégé is partially obeying the mentor, this is still disobedience. As a mentor, do not be alarmed or offended by the protégés actions. Jesus experienced the same thing in Luke 5:4-8 with the disciples when He told them to cast their nets and they only cast one net.

---

[158] Matt H. Evans, "Course 18: Leadership," July 16, 2012, www.exinfm.com/training/pdfiles/course18.pdf

The mentor will have to know when to say when. When is enough, enough? Remember, the mentor sets the tone for the mentoring relationship. Just as a parent sets boundaries for their children, the mentor will have to set boundaries for their protégé. When the protégé operates outside of those boundaries, the mentor will have to address it accordingly. The mentor will have to make difficult decisions regarding the mentoring

As a leader, are you living in a fish bowl with a skewed vision or perception of the people around you, to include your protégé?

relationship. This will include knowing when the lines of the relationship have blurred and become too personal. When the mentoring relationship becomes too personal, it is easy to lose sight of the purpose of the relationship. Sometimes leaders lose sight of their responsibility as a leader. Call it a character flaw. I simply see it as a human condition. Just as we are told, "All have sinned and fallen short of the glory of God,"[159] people must realize their imperfections. This should encourage leaders to be more

---

[159] Romans 3:23

cognizant of the role they play in the lives of their followers. What followers learn from leaders is what they see leaders doing. Think of it in terms of living in a fish bowl. This fish bowl often skews the vision or perception of the protégé, depending on how far away their vantage point is from you.[160] What kind of "birds-eye" view is the protégé getting of the mentor? Is the mentor living in a fishbowl, with their intentions skewed by distance?

Finally, it will be tempting to skip around in the model. When this is done, the effectiveness of the model is limited. Follow the model in order. As human beings, we grow, mature, and evolve in a particular span of time. The same principle applies to the mentoring relationship. What happens when a person's body, to include their organs, fails to develop properly? An abnormality or defect occurs. This affects the appearance of the person's body and / or how the person's body functions. When you skip around the model, it affects the effectiveness of the model and can complicate the mentoring relationship to the extent you will

---

[160] Linda Klebe Trevino, Michael Brown, and Laura Pincus Hartman, "A Qualitative Investigation of Perceived Executive Ethical Leadership: Perceptions from Inside and Outside the Executive Suite," *Human Relations* 56, no. 5: 2003, doi: 10.1177/0018726703056001448

struggle to identify where you are in the mentoring relationship.

At times, it can be a challenge to determine where you are in your mentoring relationship. Having an understanding of where your mentoring relationship is will help you determine how to proceed. In addition, it will help you determine how far the relationship has developed and how far it needs to go in order to reach the pre-established goals set for the relationship.

The Premature Stage

Be the one who nurtures and builds. Be the one who has an understanding and a forgiving heart one who looks for the best in people. Leave people better than you found them. ~ Marvin J. Ashton

When a woman is pregnant, a certain amount of time must pass before she can give birth to a healthy baby. She must properly care for herself, particularly in the area of nutrition. Her diet and lifestyle heavily affect the child's growth and development. The last thing the woman or her physician wants is for the child to be born prematurely. There are hosts of risks involved, to include death. Therefore, the physician does whatever is necessary to keep the baby from being born prematurely.

In the Premature Stage of the mentoring relationship, the mentor is the mother and the physician. It is the mentor's responsibility, should they decide to move forward with the relationship, to nurture the protégé, because, in this stage, the protégé is going to need a lot of attention. This may seem harsh, but just as a woman must decide if she wants to move forward in her pregnancy, the mentor must decide if this relationship is a good fit for them and the protégé. With a pregnancy, there are hosts of reasons why it may be necessary to terminate it. There could be adverse risks to the mother and the child, including the possibility of death. Sometimes this is due to an abnormality in the growth and development of the fetus.

The mentoring relationship, even at this stage, can be abnormal. The relationship is developing, and the mentor have to decide whether it is wise to pursue it. In this stage, it is critical the mentor and protégé communicate. Interviews are vital, so the mentor and the protégé can get the necessary information needed to make an informed decision. Just as the physician provides the mother with the necessary information she needs to make an informed decision about her future and that of her unborn child, the same principle applies here. As the physician, the mentor must do their homework and research. Evaluate what is going on. Interviews will be instrumental at this stage. The interview process gives the mentor the core information they need to make an informed decision. Here the mentor finds out what the protégé's core values are, what their goals are, and who they are (especially when they think no one is looking). The mentor, also, finds out a few things about themselves, particularly what they are willing to risk for the sake of this relationship. Without this information, it is difficult to make an informed decision. Ira Chaleff believes this "validates the purpose and determines how we will and how we won't pursue it."[161]

The protégé has just as much involvement and input in this stage as the mentor. Remember, learning is a two-way street, just as communication is a two-way street.

During the informational interview, be prepared. Have a set of expectations. Just like a job interview, the mentor is looking for specific things in a candidate. The mentor should have specific things they look for in a protégé. In the initial interview or conversation, the mentor wants to get past the "cliché" conversation – hellos and general pleasantries. The goal is to get to the "meat." The questions should not be subjective in nature. The goal is get a substantial response from them. Avoid "yes" and "no"

---

[161] Ira Chaleff, *The Courageous Follower 3rd Edition* (San Francisco, CA: Berrett-Koehler Publishers, Inc.), 2009

questions. Keep it brief. If the mentor cannot gather what they need in 30 minutes or less (at this stage), don't move forward. If the person sought you out, they should have an idea of what they want, what they can or cannot bring to the table, and what they expect to learn from you. The mentor should know within this span of time if their values and expectations will align with or match this particular individual. Where do you begin? Denny Strigl suggests a few things to find out:[162]

1. How do they see things, i.e. their perspective on their world?
2. What do they believe in or what's important to them?
3. What is their attitude or outlook toward the people and setting around them?
4. What is their view and pattern of thinking?

From the information gathered in the initial meeting, the mentor should be able to decide whether to pursue the relationship. Should the mentor decide to move forward, the mentor must understand and be clear on what their motives are. BE HONEST. A mentoring relationship is a

---

[162] Denny F. Strigl, *Managers, Can You Hear Me Now?* (New York, NY: McGraw-Hill), 2011.

two-way street. If the mentor thinks they won't learn from their protégé, the mentor is misinformed. While the mentor is developing the protégé, the mentor will find they will grow and develop as well. Secondly, it is going to take work. Mentoring someone is not an easy task, so the mentor should not enter into it lightly. Just as becoming a parent is a great responsibility, so is becoming a mentor. Parents form bonds with their children. The best mentors do the same, because they are invested in the life of this person.

Is This the Right Fit?

One of the difficult things about mentoring relationships is determining if it is the right fit. Here, we can look at a method human resource professionals use when matching candidates with their organization. When thinking about engaging in a mentoring relationship, the mentor should consider the values of the protégé prior to even accepting the responsibility. If the values of the protégé conflict with the mentor's personal values, why would the mentor position themselves (or the protégé) for such conflict? Part of the issues people have (or find themselves) in relationships is the fact their core values conflict with that of the other individual involved in the relationship. I am not speaking in regards to values that change due to a lifestyle change, i.e. salvation, death of a spouse, etc. Personal experiences can influence an individual's values.

Human resource professionals refer to the congruence of a person's beliefs and values with the culture, norms, and values of an organization as 'person-organization fit'.[163] This same principle can apply to the mentoring relationship. Today, people are desperate to find work; thus, they take what they can get rather than take the time to find the organization that aligns with who they are and the skills they have to offer. People are engaging in coaching relationships in an effort to improve something about themselves, but some (I dare say most) do not take the time to determine whether the person they are soliciting help from can ¹help them and ²has similar values. Why is this important? The Bible declares in Amos 3:3, "How can

---

[163] Charles Handler, "The value of person-organization fit" *Build an Interview,* June 2, 2012
http://www.buildaninterview.com/the_value_of_person_organization_f it.asp

two walk together unless they agree?" Accordingly, protégés should consider the prospective mentor's values during the initial meeting.

In the event the organization is matching individuals and said individuals do not have input in the decision, it is necessary for human resources to align the right leader with the right employee. Skipping the needs assessment process will only lead to frustration and an unsuccessful mentoring relationship. If you pair a leader who is laissez-faire and very hands-off with an employee who is new to the organization and is a kinesthetic learner, this is not going to fair well for the leader or the employee. Frustration is likely to be high on both ends. The leader will be frustrated because the needs of the employee exceed his/her expectations as a leader. The employee will be frustrated because the leader is not meeting their needs. This could lead to feelings of helplessness. Helplessness leads to alienation, which leads to confusion. From here, the employee may feel the leader does not care about them, which in turn could lead to the employee voluntarily terminating their employment.

There is an old saying, "People do not leave organizations; they leave managers." As of 2013, the Department of Labor Statistics reported the average tenure of an employee is 1.5 years. The Washington Post reported results from a LinkedIn survey that said the second reason people cited for leaving their organizations was that they wanted better leadership from senior management.[164] We can see how important it is for people's values to align with the people and organizations with which they desire to engage. In order to determine this, both parties must engage in open communication.

Open Communication

Open communication may seem like a "no brainer;" however, many people really do not know what it is. What is open communication? It is when both (or all, depending on how many people are present) are able to express ideas. Meaning, one person is not dominating or dictating the conversation. Everyone involved is able to share. When

---

[164] Jenna McGregor, "Why People Really Leave Their Jobs," *Washington Post*, March 18, 2014
http://www.washingtonpost.com/blogs/on-leadership/wp/2014/03/18/why-people-really-leave-their-jobs/

everyone is able to share, it creates an environment of mutual understanding.

Open communication establishes trust. David Hassell, CEO of 15Five, argues, "Trust grows over time and is based on individual members of a team making and keeping commitments, as well as being vulnerable with one another ... Relationships are then built upon through continued open, honest communication."[165] Open communication also enhances engagement. The more you talk, the more you discover. When the mentor shows the protégé they are interested in learning about them holistically, it makes the protégé feel as though the mentor cares about them. In turn, the protégé is open to the mentor's direction and is more inclined to follow-through with the mentor's recommendations.

It is critical the mentor and protégé establish a protocol for addressing grievances.

---

[165] David Hassell, "Open Communication: Vital to Business Success," *American Management Association*, March 25, 2013, http://www.amanet.org/training/articles/Open-Communication-Vital-to-Business-Success.aspx

In order for open communication to work, the mentor must be committed to open communication. Additionally, both parties must be positive. Be clear. Both the mentor and protégé need to know what you are doing and, more importantly, why you are doing it. Both the mentor and protégé must acknowledge any diversity between them and talk about it. Last, there will be times when the mentor and protégé will not agree with each other. The protégé may have a grievance with the mentor and the mentor a grievance with the protégé. Establish a protocol for addressing these grievances. Without this, moving forward in the mentoring relationship is unlikely. It will also hinder the tone of the relationship.

Set the Tone

What does it mean to "set the tone?" Think about an event you have attended. How did that event make you feel? Did you feel welcomed or invited when you arrived? Were you comfortable? If you were listening to a speaker, did the speaker make you feel engaged? Did you feel valued? Did you feel as though the host honored your time by being on time? Did you feel as though the host took as much interest in you as you took interest in them? Did they treat you with respect? This is what I mean by "set the tone."

The mentor is responsible for ensuring the prospective protégé is welcomed and comfortable. This starts with being on time! The Bible admonishes us to "redeem the time" (see Ephesians 5:16a). What does this mean? The Greek word for redeem is *exagorazo* (ex-ag-or-ad'-zo). It means to buy up, i.e. ransom, to rescue from loss (improve opportunity). The Greek word for time is *kairos* (kahee-ros'), which means an occasion, i.e. set or proper time – always, opportunity, (convenient, due) season, (due, short, while) time, a while. In regards to meeting your prospective protégé, to redeem their time, you are maximizing the time allotted for the occasion or opportunity to improve him or her in some manner.

Have you ever heard, "Time is money?" How do you feel when you have an appointment and the other person does not honor your time by being on time? It says to you that they do not value you or your time. Can you get the time you waited back? Matthew Henry's Concise Commentary declares, "Time is a talent given us by God, and it is misspent and lost when not employed according to his design. If we have lost our time heretofore, we must double our diligence for the future."

Greet the prospective protégé appropriately. Listen to them, and while listening to them, listen to understand. Be objective and not judgmental. It also necessary to be optimistic. Think positively about the opportunity to mentor this individual. The mentor must show the protégé they are interested in what they (the protégé) is saying. The mentor must be open-minded and treat the protégé with respect. Be willing to share information. Remember, in this stage, the mentor is gathering information and making a decision whether to become this person's mentor.

If the mentor decides the relationship is a good fit and chooses to become the protégé's mentor, the mentor must be clear on what their expectations are. Set boundaries for the relationship. What kind of boundaries should be set? Boundaries vary based upon the need. However, here are a few recommended boundaries:[166]

1. Confidentiality

---

[166] W. Brad Johnson, and Charles R. Ridley, The Elements of Mentoring (New York, NY: PALGRAVE MACMILLAN), 2004: 69

2. Appropriate mediums or contexts for interaction
3. Frequency of contact
4. Acceptability of communication by phone (work and home) and email
5. Rules governing socializing
6. A strategy for handling uncomfortable dual roles (as mentor and supervisor)[167]

Open and honest communication between mentor and protégé is essential at this stage.

The mentor must be honest with their new protégé. It will be wise not to dominate the conversation at this point. This may come across to the protégé that the mentor is a dictator and not someone who will collaborate with them. Create an environment where there is open communication. As questions are asked, the protégé should be asking the mentor questions. This information will help the mentor and the protégé as they determine the objectives of the relationship.

---

[167] This is in the case of an organizational mentoring relationship.

Establish Milestones for the Mentoring Relationship

Habakkuk 2:2 admonishes to write the vision and make it plain so the person who reads it may run with it. The Hebrew word for "run" is yā-rūs (yaw-rutz): to run (for whatever reason, especially to rush) - to break down, divide speedily, footman, guard, bring hastily, (make) run (away, through), post. Writing a vision for the mentoring relationship may seem basic, but it is needed to provide direction for the relationship. The mentor and protégé need to *see* where the mentoring relationship is going. Therefore, establish clear objectives for the mentoring relationship. An objective is the result the mentor and protégé aim to achieve within a specified time. I prefer the term "milestones." Why? By definition, a milestone marks a *significant* change or stage in development. The basis of a mentoring relationship is development. Whichever term used, the mentor and protégé must determine what they are for the relationship.

When creating milestones, the mentor and protégé want to make sure they are flexible. Life is not black and white. It is filled with gray areas. Every situation we face in life requires flexibility at some point. Setting milestones help to measure the effectiveness of the relationship, especially when it comes to the Assessment Stage of the relationship. In order to proceed, break the milestones down into three distinctions:

1. Short-term – achieved in less than 1 year
2. Intermediate – achieved within 1 - 5 years
3. Long-term – achieved within 5 – 7 years

Both the mentor and protégé should have input in creating the milestones. The milestones may be broad, but they need to be measurable. An example of a milestone may be, *"Within the next year, improve public speaking skills."* The purpose of the milestones is to be able to measure the effectiveness of the relationship. They need to be something the mentor and the protégé can achieve or attain. Therefore, be realistic about the milestones. It is perfectly acceptable to reach high; however, you do not want to reach so high the milestones are unrealistic or unattainable. Set specific timelines for the milestones. In the above example, both the mentor and the protégé can achieve this milestone. The mentor provides resources for the protégé to achieve it. For instance, the mentor may have the protégé participate in their local Toastmasters group. Think about the milestones in terms of baby steps. Each are achieved one step at a time, often in small steps.

Where Do You Begin?

A great place to begin is by setting goals. By setting goals, the milestones are streamlined and they are more defined. The goals set by the mentor and protégé need to be SMART (specific, measurable, attainable, realistic, and timely). An example of a SMART goal may be, *"Within the next six months, facilitate at least one free, one-hour time management seminar at the local library."* After setting SMART goals, proceed to write down action steps. Action steps tell you how to proceed with the milestones and goals.

Establishing a Plan of Action to Address the Protégé's Needs

In the previous chapter, we discussed the importance of the protégé knowing what their needs are. This is the information they will bring to the table, so to speak, to help the mentor establish a plan of action. In the event the protégé is unsure of what their needs are or is vague about their needs, the mentor will need to spend time determining what the protégé's needs are. Without this information, the mentor will not be able to establish a plan of action. As discussed in the previous chapter, there are several methods for determining what a person's needs are. You can begin with a simple questionnaire, use an online tool, or start with a SWOT analysis. For details on these methods, refer to the previous chapter, "Choosing a Mentor."

The action plan should include solutions to address the specific needs the protégé has outlined. During the initial discussion, it is likely the mentor identified additional needs. These should be included in the action plan as well. In order to establish the action plan, the mentor may need to evaluate the root cause of the protégé's needs. For instance, are some of the protégé's needs cultural traditions? Understanding the root cause will help the mentor determine the best way to approach the need. The mentor will also need to determine with the protégé if there are any constraints to their needs. Constraints are any factors that would prevent the mentor from addressing their needs. For instance, are there financial obligations the protégé has that would prevent them from addressing their need? Is lack of education an issue that is preventing them from addressing one of their needs? With this information, the mentor is able to discover the resources that are available or may be available to help the protégé address certain needs.

The action plan should be clear and detailed. It should state what you are doing; who is responsible for completing the task; when the task is to be completed; and what the expected outcome will be. Using our SMART goal example, here are some recommended action steps:

1. Over the next 3 months, create the time management seminar.
2. Within 1 month after establishing the goal, contact the local library to discuss the seminar. Here you will find out the policies and procedures as well as financial costs (if any). You will also schedule the seminar.
3. Within 1 month of the seminar date, promote the seminar.
4. Conduct the seminar.

5. Within 1 week following the seminar, review feedback from the seminar.

Now that the action plan is in place, the mentoring relationship can begin. It is important to remember to document the relationship. This will help the mentor measure the effectiveness of their plan as well as their leadership. It will also help them determine if their protégé is reaching the milestones set when the mentor and protégé discussed the objectives of the relationship. From this point, the relationship unfolds in stages.

The Infant Stage

We must open the doors of opportunity. But we must also equip our people to walk through those doors. ~ Lyndon B. Johnson

Now that you have decided to pursue the mentoring relationship, the training begins. Infants need 24/7 care. It is seemingly unending. You rest when you get a chance. You are on-call all of the time. You will bottle-feed, burp, change diapers, and rock the child to sleep. You work to get the child on a schedule. When my sister had her first child, she visited a clinical nurse who specialized in helping first-time mothers learn how to breast-feed and how to get the baby on a feeding schedule that aligns with your time zone. She told my sister, "When babies are born, they are born on Australian time." So you have to get the baby adjusted to the schedule you want for them as a parent. In this case, the United States. As a mentor, this is what you will do. The mentoring relationship is the equivalent of a single-parent relationship. Your protégé will need you just as much as a baby needs a parent.

As a parent equips and nurtures the child with proper nutrition and clothing, a mentor will follow suit. The mentor will "arm" their protégé with the necessary tools they need to be successful. This may include recommended reading, seminars, and conferences. The mentor will likely speak with their protégé daily, sometimes several times a day. The mentor will be extremely hands-on in this stage.

As the child grows, the lessons the parent teaches them shift. They begin to recognize shapes, learn how to walk, and let us not forget the joy of potty training. There is a sense of pride and overwhelming joy, though, as the parent watches their child grow and develop. The parent, also, recognize the lessons and values they want to instill in their child. The parent finds ways to discipline their child so they know what to do and what not to do. Playing near electrical sockets is a definite "no," but the child does not know this. The parent has to teach them. The same principle applies when the child wants to play with chords, experiment with shaving (when they think they are old enough), etc. Children are a blank canvas. What a parent chooses to paint for them is solely up to the parent.

A mentors protégé is a blank canvas but not in the same sense as that of a child. This person is coming to the mentor with ideals, cultural disparities, and other preconceived notions in their mind. They must be willing to forgo most of that if they expect to get the most out of the mentoring relationship. The mentor leaves a footprint in this person's life. This person is learning from the mentor: what the mentor says and what the mentor is not saying. They are observing everything the mentor says and does. Therefore, who the mentor is when no one is looking is just as important as the things the mentor says. This is what is known as "character."

As a protégé, remember you are just as much responsible for your growth and development as the mentor. The mentor serves to equip you, but you must ensure they are equipping you in the right areas. What do you want painted on your blank canvas?

Bill Hybels defines character as who we are. He says, "Character cannot be developed through good resolutions and checklists. It usually requires a lot of hard work, a little pain and years of faithfulness before any of the virtues are consistently noticeable in us."[168] Character is what every

---

[168] Bill Hybels, *Who You Are When No One's Looking*, (Downers

parent is instilling in their children from the moment they enter into this world. Everything a parent says and does influences the child's character development. As a mentor, this is the same principle. Over time, the mentor instills certain character traits in their protégés. One of the best ways to do this is by example, which is discussed in the next stage.

Do You Trust Me?

While I am certain there is any number of methods to encourage better followership, I ascertain it begins with relationship. Most leader / follower relationships hinge upon a level of trust. Ira Chaleff states, "Trust is essential in the leader-follower relationship if followers are to serve and influence the leader and organization. Yet sometimes it is elusive."[169] People tend to forget there are (at a minimum) two personalities, two entities, two individuals involved in a relationship. Stephen Covey says we should recognize that each relationship has two trust accounts.[170] This says to me that you have to give as much as you receive.

Grove, IL: InterVarsity Press), 1987.
[169] Ira Chaleff, *The Courageous Follower 3rd Edition* (San Francisco, CA: Berrett-Koehler Publishers, Inc) 2009.
[170] Stephen R. Covey, *The Speed of Trust: The One Thing That Changes Everything.* (New York, NY: Free Press), 2006.

Trust is earned and is not a commodity to be traded or sold. It is like time, not easy to come by. Once it is lost, it is a struggle to get it back. Chip Bell suggests trust is born out of humility.[171] "Humility has a special role in relationships in which there is an unequal distribution of power: Trust is the equalizer."[172] If we apply this principle to a person's relationship with Christ, perhaps the person can "lead by example" and become the living Word that others will choose to follow. Kathy Kram believed when mentors are role models guiding their protégés through exemplary values, behaviors, and achievements are likely to gain the respect and trust of their protégés.[173] Simply put, the protégé will learn from watching the mentor.

This is how children learn. If you observe a child, they imitate what they see others do. Andrew Meltzoff conducted a study with 14-month old infants. In the study, the infants watched adults perform particular actions on six objects. The person demonstrating the actions never spoke

---

[171] Chip R. Bell, *Managers as Mentors: Building Partnerships for Learning 2nd Edition* (San Francisco, CA: Berrett-Koehler Publishers, Inc.), 2002.

[172] Ibid, 46

[173] Kathy Kram, *Mentoring at Work: Developmental Relationships in Organizational Life* (Glenview, IL: Scott, Foresman), 1985.

or advised the children to imitate them. In the study, the infants were not allowed to touch the objects. They could only watch what the adult did. After 1-week, the 14-month old infants were allowed to touch the objects. As a result, 67% of the infants imitated what the adult did.[174]

Children can have a large capacity for trust or mistrust. It depends on the parent. Erik Erikson, a German psychologist, identified eight stages of psychosocial development in people from infancy to adulthood. In his first stage, Erikson believed that patterns of trust or mistrust are formed that control, or influence, a person's actions or interactions for the rest of their life.[175] An infant's trust level increases (or decreases) based upon the parent's interaction with them. An infant depends on the parent to provide for their basic needs. When the parent provides for the child's basic needs (food, love, affection, and stimulation), the child's trust increases. This increases the child's attachment to the parent.

---

[174] Andrew N. Meltzoff, "Born to Learn: What Infants Learn from Watching Us" [PDF document], 1999, http://ilabs.washington.edu/meltzoff/pdf/99Meltzoff_BornToLearn.pdf

[175] Erik H. Erikson, *Childhood and Society* (New York, NY: WW Horton and Company, Inc.), 1950

This same principle applies in the Infant Stage of the mentoring relationship. The protégé's trust towards the mentor will strengthen as the mentor addresses the protégé's needs. The more the mentor addresses the protégé's needs, the more attached and the more engaged the protégé will become. As the relationship deepens, both the mentor and the protégé learn.

The Learning Stage

In learning you will teach, and in teaching you will learn. ~ Phil Collins

Following the same concept as we have, there comes a point in the parent-child relationship when a parent releases their child to learn from what they have shown them. From the moment a child enters this world, they begin to learn. Jean Piaget was a developmental biologist who spent the majority of his life observing and recording the intellectual abilities of infants, children and adolescents. He observed that children from ages 0-24 months learn everything from reflexes to problem solving. This is the Sensory Motor Stage. The Pre-Operational Stage occurs between the ages of 2 and 7. Here the child's speech develops more. It is egocentric in nature, because it is more social. The next stage is Concrete Operational. This occurs between the ages of 7 and 12. Here the child is able to place things in a logical order and is able to do some concrete problem solving. Lastly, there is the Formal Operations Stage. This stage occurs at the age of 12 and progresses throughout life. In this stage, Piaget observes that "thought becomes more abstract, incorporating the principles of formal logic."[176]

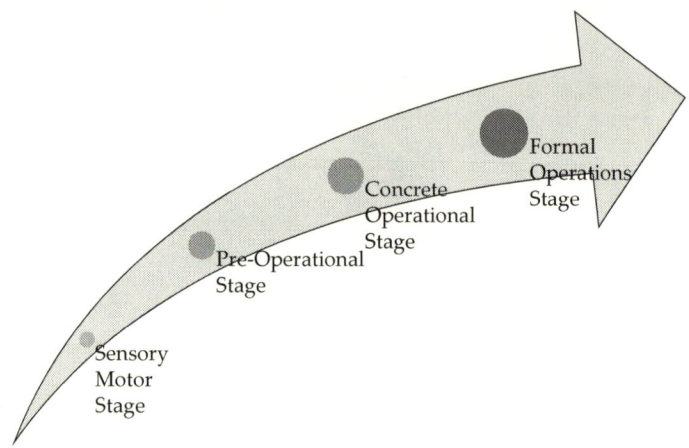

Children learn in a variety of ways, and school is one of those methods. When a parent sends their child to day care, the child learns from that environment. They learn to balance what they see in pre-school from what they see at home. As the child grows and matriculates through the various grades, they build upon that foundation.

As a mentor, the protégé will go through a similar experience. In this particular stage, both the mentor and protégé are learning. The mentor is learning their protégé's

---

[176] "Stages Of Intellectual Development In Children And Teenagers," *Child Development Institute*, 1999-2013, http://childdevelopmentinfo.com/child-development/piaget/

capacity for growth and their retention span. The protégé is learning the mentor's leadership style as well as how to grow under the mentor's tutelage. The protégé is learning what to do as well as what not to do based on what they observe from their mentor. They, also, learn from the reading materials the mentor assigns.

    The different learning styles will come into play here. The mentor will begin to see if the learning style their protégé says they have actually aligns with what they do. Both the mentor and protégé will need to be patient and flexible in this stage. Think about a child learning to walk for the first time. A parent is excited for the child's first steps. It is a major milestone. While the parent is confident in the child's ability to gain enough balance to take that first step, the child is not as confident as the parent is. Faith is frightening, because it requires a person to move in the realm of the unknown. After all, faith is the substance of things *hoped* for and the evidence of things *not seen*.[177] However, with faith, the more it is exercised, the more confident a person is in God. The more the protégé learns from their mentor and the resources the mentor provides

---

[177] Hebrews 11:1

them with, the more confident they will become in the mentor and those resources. Trust builds this confidence.[178]

Since I keep referring to resources, you may be wondering what kind of resources the mentor may recommend for their protégé. These resources will depend upon the protégé's needs. Some basic resources include, but are not limited to,

- Time Management
- Tips for Overcoming Procrastination
- Stress Management
- Tips for Overcoming Anxiety

The academic community uses different learning strategies to help students learn. Some of these learning strategies can be used in the mentoring relationship. The Center for Research on Learning at the University of Kansas offers some excellent learning strategies. I particularly was drawn to their strategies for effectively interacting with others as well as their strategies for motivation. Below are some of their strategies by category:[179]

---

[178] By definition, trust is the belief that someone or something is reliable.

[179] "Learning Strategies," *University of Kansas Center for Research*

- Strategies for Effectively Interacting with Others
  - SLANT
  - Cooperative Thinking Strategies
    - THINK Strategy (Problem Solving)
    - LEARN Strategy (Learning Critical Information)
    - BUILD Strategy (Decision Making)
    - SCORE Skills: Social Skills for Cooperative Groups
    - Teamwork Strategy
  - Community Building
    - Focusing Together
    - Following Instructions Together
    - Organizing Together
    - Taking Notes Together
    - Talking Together
- Strategies for Motivation
  - Self-Advocacy Strategy
  - Possible Selves

In their strategies for effectively interacting with others, they have a class called SLANT. This class helps students learn how to use appropriate posture and to activate their thinking (among other things). What does posture have to do with anything? Posture has *everything* to do with it!

---

on Learning, 2014, http://www.ku-crl.org/sim/strategies.shtml

Remember earlier in the book when I talked about microexpressions and body language? In their book, *My Doctor Never Told Me That!*, Christine and Madison Spurlock argue that our posture can tell a lot about what is going on in a person's mind. A person's posture reflects their confidence. For example, a person's back straight to create an erect posture is a sign of confidence.[180] Richard Brennan believes changing your posture will change the way you think.[181] Remember my discussion on open communication? Well, posture has a role in that as well! According to Patricia Barbato,

> Your posture will also say a lot to the other person. Are you slouched in your chair and not making eye contact? This sends a clear message that you are not interested in what the other person has to say, even before anything is said. An open, relaxed posture will set the tone that you are available and open to the communication.[182]

---

[180] Sharon Sayler, *What Your Body Says (And How to Master the Message): Inspire, Influence, Build Trust, and Create Lasting Business Relationships* (Hoboken, NJ: John Wiley and Sons, Inc.), 2011: 6

[181] Richard Brennan, *Change Your Posture, Change Your Life: How the Power of the Alexander Technique Can Combat Back Pain, Tension and Stress* (London, UK: Duncan Baird Publishers), 2012.

[182] Patricia Barbato, *Inspire Your Career: Strategies for Success in Your First Years at Work* (Ontario, Canada: Insomniac Press), 2010: 83.

In the Learning Stage, the protégé is not the only person learning. The mentor learn a great deal about their leadership abilities as well as when and how to adjust their style based on the needs of their protégé and followers. The person's capacity to mentor and lead others will be exposed. The leader will definitely learn a lot about themselves, especially as they transition into the next stage: the Living Stage.

The Living Stage

> *Life is not a solo act. It's a huge collaboration, and we all need to assemble around us the people who care about us and support us in times of strife. ~*
> Tim Gunn

We continue the mentoring relationship in the living stage as a reflection of the parent-child relationship. Here, the child has graduated from high school and is venturing off to pursue their life's goals. This may be a desire to attend college, enlist in the military, or work a full-time job. At this point in the child's life, the parent is not as hands-on. They allow the child to "spread their wings."

The mentor's hands-on experience with their protégé lessens in this stage. The mentor "releases" the protégé, so to speak, to explore their goals and aspirations. The mentor looks on from a safe distance, checking in periodically. This is where the "rubber meets the road" and the mentor gets to see if their protégé has learned anything from the resources, examples, and experiences presented to them thus far. The lessons they have learned up to this point will help the protégé maneuver through life's challenges, both personally and professionally. I am not saying the protégé does not have any hands-on experience up to this point. Their life is not on hold; however, the level of involvement the mentor has in their life changes at this point.

The mentor's role is to be supportive. Sometimes the mentor will need to step in and give advice even when the protégé does not ask for it. Just like children who are "first time" adults may overextend themselves and may not realize they are in over their heads, the same applies to the protégé. Sometimes parents step in and help their children even when they do not ask. Why? Because the parent sees they need it. It is not that they do not believe they are capable, but the parent sees the consequences of a poor decision – even if not making a decision leads to the same consequence. Failure to make a decision is still a decision. Sometimes people are not sure what to do.

The mentor must be careful not to become overbearing and overstep their boundaries. While the mentor may be passionate about their protégé's success, the mentor must know when to take a step back. The mentor does not want to become pushy. This can, in turn, push the protégé in the opposite direction or cause the protégé to want to terminate the mentoring relationship, because the mentor's passion caused too much conflict. If the mentor continually pushes their protégé's limits, it's likely the mentor will rub them the wrong way.[183]

Remember, the mentor's role is to *serve* the protégé. The mentor is not there to *dictate*. Remember the boundaries set earlier in the relationship. This will help keep things in perspective as the mentoring relationship grows and develops. Parents set boundaries for their children. A parent would not allow their 13-year-old daughter, for instance, to come home at 2:00 in the morning. Nor would a parent allow their 10-year-old daughter to wear makeup and start dating boys. Boundaries are being established.

Boundaries are necessary and healthy for a relationship to flourish!

God established boundaries early in creation. Think about light and darkness. Darkness has boundaries. It

---

[183] John C. Maxwell, *The 360° Leader: Developing Your Influence from Anywhere in the Organization* (Nashville, TN: Thomas Nelson), 2005: 27.

cannot exist in the presence of light. Think about the sky and the waters. The sky has boundaries and so do the waters. The waters cannot extend into the sky nor can the sky descend into the waters. Think about land-based animals in relationship to water-based animals. Water-based animals cannot survive on land any more than land-based animals can survive in water. A fish out of water will suffocate, because it is outside of its boundary. Even the seasons have boundaries. Jesus showed us how to set boundaries when He drove the sellers out of the temple, when He turned potential followers away,[184] when He left the disciples to spend time alone with God, and when He rebuked the Pharisees for their hypocrisy. Boundaries are necessary and healthy for a relationship to flourish!

In the Living Stage, the protégé is not alone. The mentor is still there to guide the protégé, but this is where the mentor steps back to see what the protégé has learned. How much have they grown? What do they still need to work on? What is the next step for them? This step gives the mentor the information they need to transition into the next stage: the assessment.

---

[184] Read Mark 5. After He healed the demoniac, the man wanted to become a disciple. Jesus refused him and told him to return to his people.

The Assessment Stage

A truthful evaluation of yourself gives feedback for growth and success. ~ Brenda Johnson Padgitt

This stage is self-explanatory. Just as a manager evaluates their employee's performance, the mentor needs to evaluate the mentoring relationship to see what adjustments need to be made (if any). The mentor spends time talking with the protégé and the two of you compare notes (so to speak) about the relationship. You look at the relationship from the very beginning and discuss your milestones, both positive and negative. These milestones are measured against the ones created in the Premature Stage. The negative milestones are those that occurred during the course of the relationship. These are any setbacks in the relationship due to moments of distrust, unbelief, uncertainty, fear, or lack of participation. Core values and goals that were set forth in the beginning are reviewed to see whether they have been achieved. Any hindrances or obstacles to the success of the relationship are discussed.

At this stage of the mentoring relationship, another decision is necessary. Just as in the beginning the decision whether to pursue the relationship had to be made, it is at this stage the decision to continue or terminate the relationship is made. This will be based on the feedback from the assessment. There are different types of assessments you can use.

One of the first assessments you want to explore is feedback from the protégé on the mentor's leadership. Peter Northouse offers a Leadership Trait Questionnaire (LTQ) in his book *Leadership Theory and Practice*. Northouse asserts, "The LTQ quantifies the perceptions of the individual leader and selected observers, such as subordinates or peers. It measures an individual's traits and points the individual to the areas in which he or she may have special strengths or weaknesses."[185] Likewise, the mentor may want to do a self-check on their leadership to see what adjustments they need to make. Maxwell offers one in his article for *The Voice* entitled, "A Leadership Check-up". In it he said, "A vital leader seldom waits for failure before

---

[185] Peter G. Northouse, *Leadership: Theory and practice 4th Edition* (Thousand Oaks, CA: Sage Publications), 2007: 32

appraising his or her leadership skills." He introduced eight questions to help evaluate leadership strengths and weaknesses.[186]

1. How and where do I have influence?
2. Where can I improve my people skills?
3. Do I have a positive outlook?
4. Do I see evidence of growth in self-discipline?
5. Do I have a proven track record of success in my field?
6. How are my problem-solving skills?
7. Do I refuse to accept the status quo?
8. Do I have a big-picture mindset?

Qualitative approaches can be used as well. Whatever method of assessment chosen, make sure the feedback collected from it limits the amount of bias. Granted it may be impossible to escape bias, since the mentor and protégé is evaluating a relationship they apart of; however, the mentor and protégé wants to protect the validity of the assessment. Find a way to turn the bias into insight.

---

[186] John C. Maxwell, "A Leadership Check-Up," *The VOICE Magazine*, 2011, http://www.thevoicemagazine.com/leadership-/leadership/a-leadership-check-up.html

Identifying When Something in the Relationship Has Changed or Shifted

People are unpredictable. It makes sense that some type of dysfunction is bound to surface during the course of the mentoring relationship. It is important to track this dysfunction and address it immediately, so it does not fester. The Bible declares it is unwise to let the sun set on your anger.[187] The reason for this is that the longer you let something go without addressing it, the angrier you become. It negatively affects your relationship. This is why I advised earlier to take notes throughout the mentoring relationship. These notes will help to identify when something in the relationship has changed or shifted. What if the notes do not present anything? There are other ways to identify when something in the relationship has changed or shifted.

One of the first things to examine is how many negative interactions outweigh the positive. What was the cause of these negative interactions? Were there external forces involved? Was it an issue with conflicting

---

[187] Ephesians 4:26

personalities? People experience growing pains. It is natural. Consider the relationship between parents and teenagers. One moment there is a strong, loving relationship and then puberty hits. The teenager is experiencing lots of angst and emotional turmoil mostly due to social challenges. Does the parent immediately divorce their child? Of course not! However, the parent does address the situation with their teenager. The parent may even punish the teenager. But they at least *talk* with their teenager.

As the protégé, you may need to address observations of your own. Be honest and non-judgmental. This is not the opportunity to point the finger and lay blame. This is the opportunity to transition the relationship into a positive direction.

In the mentoring relationship, the mentor sits down with their protégé and discusses the situation. The mentor discovers what the root cause of the issue is and addresses it accordingly. Do not play the blame game here. This can easily turn into a heated argument full of judgment. What the mentor wants to do is state their observations. Exercise open communication. What the mentor observes is not necessarily what the protégé observes. Each has differing perspectives and both perspectives need to be expressed.

If there are any destructive patterns of behavior, agree to stop the behavior immediately. Make an agreement to focus on positive behaviors. Perhaps the mentor needs to affirm their protégé more than they chasten them, even if the protégé is constantly wrong. Constructive criticism goes a long way. If a person only hears negative feedback, they are not likely to respond in a positive manner. The mentor and protégé must be careful with negative feedback as the mentor and protégé may become emotionally abusive towards one another. Some people are emotionally driven, so you must be careful to steward each other's emotions throughout the relationship. This may sound strange, but perhaps the mentor needs to determine the protégé's love language and vice versa. Gary Chapman has a series of books on the subject ranging from how to communicate in your marriage to communicating in the workplace, to include the military. In reading his work, I found appreciation (to include affirmation) to be a consistent theme. This says to me people need and value encouragement.

Many times dysfunction occurs due to poor communication. Each person may think they are communicating effectively. Remember, communication is a two-way channel. It requires a speaker and a listener. Earlier, I discussed the importance of listening to understand and not to respond. Examine the conversations shared with throughout the relationship. How often did either of you listen to respond rather than to understand? How often did you interrupt each other when the other was speaking? These are important details to note. If neither of you are allowing the other to speak freely without interruption, there is a serious communication problem. This is perhaps the root cause of the dysfunction occurring in the relationship.

Another dysfunction could be lack of trust. Remember, trust develops over time. Over time, the mentor and protégé develop confidence in each other. Along the way, something happened that caused the two to become suspicious of one another. You may be questioning each other's motives, integrity, or even capabilities. Openly communicate with each other about the lack of trust that exists in the relationship. Agree to start building trust accounts. Stephen Covey wrote about this in *The Speed of Trust*. Every relationship has two trust accounts. (I mentioned this earlier in the book.) He notes,

> The way you perceive the amount of trust in a relationship and the way the other person perceives it may be different. So it's generally wise to think of any relationship in terms of two accounts – not one – and to try to be aware of the balance in each account.[188]

Covey makes several other annotations regarding the trust account:[189]

1. Each trust account is unique.
2. All deposits and withdrawals are not created equal.
3. What constitutes a "deposit" to one person may not to another.
4. Withdrawals are typically larger than deposits.
5. Sometimes the fastest way to build trust is to stop making withdrawals.

While discussing issues surrounding trust, determine whether the trust is broken to the point of

---

[188] Stephen Covey, *The Speed of Trust* (New York, NY: Free Press), 2006: 132.
[189] Ibid, 131-132

disrepair. If this is the case, it is wise to sever the relationship. However, if the relationship can be salvaged, discuss "deal breakers" moving forward in the relationship. These are things that either of you absolutely will not allow in the relationship moving forward. These kinds of boundaries help to keep the relationship in proper perspective. Can the mentor still fulfill the protégé's needs?

Behavior patterns are another dysfunction. Annotate specific behavior patterns and discuss them openly. I recommend writing them in a list format. Then next to each behavior, write down what you would like to change about that behavior. This is a working list, much like a business plan. You want to refer back to it often to ensure the behavior is changing. It will require some trial and error as well.

Sometimes two people will agree to disagree too much. This can make the relationship toxic and dysfunctional. At some point, someone is going to have to yield to the other. Often, it should be the protégé submitting to the authority of the mentor. However, there are times when the mentor should submit to the protégé. Your protégé may have the courage to challenge your behavior as a leader when it threatens the common purpose of the relationship.[190] The mentor must be *humble* enough to submit to the protégé's feedback and adjust their behavior accordingly.

A relationship requires two people and it requires those two people to be willing to submit to each other. When dysfunction occurs, it is usually a sign of unwillingness to submit. Regardless of where the dysfunction originated, one fundamental act must be evoked: FORGIVENESS. Jesus tells us in Matthew 6:14-15,[191] "For if you forgive people their wrongdoing, your heavenly Father will forgive you as well. But if you don't forgive people, your Father will not forgive your wrongdoing."

Be humble and willing to submit to each other. It is from a place of humility where you can truly begin to receive.

Recall earlier in the PLUS analogy that prayer is essential to the mentoring relationship. If you choose not to exercise forgiveness, you hinder your prayers. The Bible is

---

[190] Ira Chaleff, *The Courageous Follower 3rd Edition* (San Francisco, CA: Berrett-Koehler Publishers), 2009: 85.
[191] Holman Christian Standard Bible, HCSB

clear in Mark 11:25-26,[192] "And whenever you stand praying, if you have anything against anyone, forgive him, so that your Father in heaven will also forgive you your wrongdoing. [But if you don't forgive, neither will your Father in heaven forgive your wrongdoing.]" Forgiveness is reinforced repeatedly throughout the Bible. Forgiveness is like a bridge. It is the connection to rebuilding and reconciliation. Unforgiveness skews your perspective of the relationship; therefore, when you evaluate the growth of the relationship, you may not see the full extent of where the relationship has gone.

Conflict Resolution

Max de Pree said, "The key elements in the art of working together are how to deal with change, how to deal with conflict, and how to reach our potential ... the needs of the team are best met when we meet the needs of individual persons." Conflict is the perceived incompatibilities by parties of the views, wishes, and desires each holds.[193] Conflict is unavoidable, especially

---
[192] Holman Christian Standard Bible, HCSB
[193] Karen A. Jehn, (1992). "The Impact Of Intragroup Conflict On Group Effectiveness: A Multi Method Examination of the Benefits

when the individuals involved come from diverse backgrounds. Unfortunately, the effects of conflict lead to dissatisfaction, uncooperative team members, demotivation, and (ultimately) loss of productivity. For these reasons, it is vitally important for the mentor to have a firm grasp on how to effectively manage and resolve conflict. The mentor sets the tone with respect to conflict – how it is introduced and how it is resolved.

Conflict can arise from different sources. The mentor and protégé may have conflict over content. This is where you disagree over what a statement or concept means.[194] The mentor and protégé may have conflict over values. There may even e conflict surrounding how you define yourselves. People define themselves based on their individual self-concept. How people define themselves is deep-rooted. Changing a person's self-perception is difficult. The mentor and protégé will face resistance in this area. One thing the mentor and protégé do not want to do is generalize or categorize each other. Categorizing each

---

and Detriments of Conflict," (Unpublished doctoral dissertation, Evanston, IL: Northwestern University).
    [194] Lowell H. Lamberton, and Leslie Minor, *Human Relations: Strategies for Success 4th Edition* (Boston, MA: McGraw Hill), 2010: 345.

other can provoke hostility or animosity.[195] Therefore, the mentor needs to know the five different styles or modes of conflict resolution according to M. Afzalur Rahim. These styles or modes of conflict resolution are:[196]

- Competing
- Accommodation
- Collaboration
- Avoiding
- Compromise

In competing, people believe goals are negatively related. Therefore, successful goal attainment makes others less likely to reach their goals.[197] Competition is characterized by high assertiveness involving the use of power to gain acceptance of one's position. Accommodation, on the other hand, is characterized by

---

[195] Oluremi B. Ayoko, and Charmine E.J. Hartel, "Cultural Diversity and Leadership: A Conceptual Model of Leader Intervention in Conflict Events in Culturally Heterogeneous Workgroups." *Cross Cultural Management: An International Journal* 13, no. 4, 2006: 348, doi: 10.1108/13527600610713431

[196] M. Afzalur Rahim, *Managing Conflict in Organizations* (New York, NY: Praeger Publishers), 1992.

[197] Jia-Chi Huang, "Unbundling Task Conflict and Relationship Conflict: The Moderating Role of Team Goal Orientation and Conflict Management" *International Journal of Conflict Management* 21, no. 3, 2010: 334-355, doi: 10.1108/10444061011063207

high cooperativeness, satisfying the other party's wishes at the expense of one's own. This promotes mutual goals, because people believe their goals are positively.[198] Collaboration involves a high combination of the competing and accommodating styles. All pertinent issues and concerns are brought out into the open in order to reach a solution that integrates all points of view. Here it is important to introduce sensitiveness to local workplace social processes in shaping the possible emergence of shared cultural meanings.[199] Avoidance is low in competing and accommodation. It involves sidestepping an issue and shying away from an open discussion about the issue. It is the attempt to smooth over conflicts and minimize

Regardless of the approach, address conflict. Do not allow conflict to go unresolved. Unresolved conflict leads to greater dysfunction, unhealthy relationships, and unproductive mentoring relationships.

---

[198] Ibid

[199] Toke Bjerregaard, Jakob Lauring and Anders Klitmoller, "A Critical Analysis Of Intercultural Communication Research In Cross-Cultural Management: Introducing Newer Developments In Anthropology," *Critical Perspectives on International Business* 5, no. 3, 2009: 207-228, doi: 10.1108/17422040910974695

discussion of them.[200] Finally, compromise involves splitting the difference with both parties giving up something to find a middle ground.

The personalities and attitudes of the mentor and protégé determine how they address conflict. If the mentor or protégé is a low conformer, someone who thinks independently, there will be difficulty. With low conformers, honesty must be tolerated. These people are typically straightforward and blunt. Tread carefully with the low conformer and not judge their behavior as stubborn. Rather, be supportive. It is likely the low conformer has a host of critical people in their life. While it may be difficult, resist the urge to force them to conform. Give them positive reinforcement relevant to what you are doing.[201]

If dealing with someone who has a problem with envy, confrontation is necessary. Openly confront them

---

[200] Jia-Chi Huang, "Unbundling Task Conflict and Relationship Conflict: The Moderating Role of Team Goal Orientation and Conflict Management," *International Journal of Conflict Management* 21, no. 3, 2010: 334-355, doi:10.1108/10444061011063207

[201] Lowell H. Lamberton, and Leslie Minor, (*Human Relations: Strategies for Success 4th Edition* (Boston, MA: McGraw Hill), 2010: 354-355.

about their envy and be willing to uncover the root of why the person is envious. It is likely this person suffers from low-self-esteem. They will need to be affirmed and built up.[202]

If dealing with someone who likes to whine and complain, listen to them but do not indulge their behavior. These people need frequent reality checks. Force them to focus on the problem rather than giving them space to complain. Do not ask them open-ended questions. This could lead to a gripe session.[203]

If addressing someone who is passive, ask them open-ended questions. Then give them time to speak. It will be tempting to fill the quiet space with small talk. Don't! This will only enable their behavior to remain passive. Set time limits when dealing with passive people.[204]

Conflict resolution requires immediate action. You do not want issues to prolong and fester. Dealing with conflict requires a leader who is adept at addressing hard problems. Dealing with conflict is like addressing an open wound. It must be handled with care. You have to apply a

---

[202] Ibid, 355-356
[203] Ibid, 356-357
[204] Ibid, 358

cleaning agent. Usually when there is an open wound, you apply Bacitracin, peroxide, or alcohol to it to avoid infection. Then you apply Neosporin and a Band-Aid. What you do not do is poor water on it or ignore it completely. In doing so, you risk infection leading to a worsening problem. Carl Honore puts it like this, "Whether it's mending a failing company, fighting corruption, tackling disease, or rebuilding a marriage, the hardest problems defy just-add-water remedies. Indeed, slapping on a Band-Aid when surgery is needed usually just makes things worse."

Evaluate the Growth

During the Premature Stage, the mentor and the protégé set milestones. Against those milestones, SMART goals were set. Here the mentor and protégé will measure the growth of the mentoring relationship against those milestones and goals. While it is likely the mentor and protégé are "checking off" their goals throughout the relationship, a panoramic view of the relationship is necessary. It helps the mentor and protégé to see just how much they have accomplished. Certain questions may be asked:

1. What are the most valuable things you have achieved throughout the relationship?
2. What would you like to change about the relationship?
3. Are there any significant goals or milestones you would like to change?
4. How can the two of you improve the way you are addressing current challenges in the relationship?
5. What do you need to keep doing or what do you need to change?

These questions will help to form the panoramic view of the mentoring relationship. Why is this helpful? Consider the story of Moses on the mountain in Exodus 17:8-16. During the war against the Amalekites, Moses *went up on a hill* with Aaron and Hur. Upon the hill, Moses saw whenever his hand was raised, the Israelites were victorious against the Amalekites. However, when his hand lowered, the Amalekites overtook the Israelites. Whenever Moses' hands were tired, Aaron and Hur would prop them up. Thus, Joshua and the Israelites were victorious over the Amalekites. Because Moses had a panoramic view of the battlefield, he was able to see what worked and what did not work. When the mentor and protégé gets a panoramic view of the mentoring relationship, they see what is working and what needs to change. Let's take a look at evaluation criteria and methods for evaluation.

Evaluation Criteria

The evaluation criteria help you directly measure your progress towards specific milestones in the mentoring relationship. Now, it is not necessary to focus on how the criterion is measured. In the next section, we will discuss methods for evaluation. The goal here is to be as specific as possible. Do not worry if there are too many criteria in place. It is a good thing to have several criteria rather than not enough. Here are a few things to consider when establishing your evaluation criteria:[205]

1. Criteria should reflect explicit performance targets.
2. Criteria should not be subjective.

---

[205] US Department of Justice, "Program Evaluation and Analysis: A Technical Guide for State and Local Governments," Washington, DC: Prepared for the US Department of Housing and Urban Development, 1978: 15-16.

3. Criteria should indicate elative accomplishments.
4. Criteria should cover all important attributes or aspects of the relationship.
5. Criteria should be acceptable to the mentor and protégé.

I want to reiterate that the mentor and protégé are comparing the milestones established earlier in the relationship with their goals. Therefore, when devising the criteria, remember that an evaluation is a comparison. Ultimately, the goal is to get a panoramic view of the mentoring relationship. Let's take a look at a few evaluation methods.

Evaluation Methods

An evaluation is nothing more than a determination of whether something you are doing is worth it or is significant. A set of standards governs the evaluation. There are three types of evaluation methods that can be used: qualitative, quantitative, or a combination of the two. It depends on what is being evaluated. When using qualitative evaluation, the focus is on words rather than numbers as in quantitative evaluation. Therefore, open-ended questions are used in a qualitative approach. In a quantitative approach, closed-ended questions are used.[206] Think of qualitative evaluations in terms of behavior, perception, and perspective. The qualitative method will likely be used the most. However, if financial milestones and goals are in place, obviously a quantitative method will be used.

How do you determine which method to use? Well, begin by asking, "Will the information we seek in this process be best supplied by survey results, objective data, etc. (quantitative data) or from interviews (qualitative data)?" Perhaps a combination of the two will be beneficial. This is perfectly acceptable.

Another way to approach the evaluation method is to create a grid with four columns. The grid includes a specific milestone or goal, the result of that milestone or goal, and the timeframe of the milestone or goal. In the final column, list the

When establishing the evaluation criteria, keep in mind this is a joint effort between the mentor and protégé.

---

[206] John W. Creswell, *Research Design: Qualitative, Quantitative, and Mixed Methods Approaches 3rd Edition* (Los Angeles, CA: Sage Publications), 2009: 3.

evaluation method how you tracked it. For example, using our previous example regarding improving public speaking skills, below is how the grid will look.

Milestone	Result	Timeframe	Evaluation Method
Improve public speaking skills	Conduct one-hour seminar at local library	Within 1st year of the relationship	Calendar

Once again, we see how important it is for both the mentor and protégé to keep detailed notes of the mentoring relationship. This information will be vital to the assessment process. Without this information, the mentor and protégé will spend excess time brainstorming on previous events in the relationship rather than on the quality of the relationship. Remember, the mentor and protégé wants a panoramic view of the relationship and now they want to evaluate that view. The focus is on how successful the relationship has been. This will determine how the mentor and protégé proceed in the relationship.

Determining When to Terminate the Relationship

The purpose of assessing the mentoring relationship is to see if it is on target with expected milestones. Another purpose is to evaluate whether it is a healthy relationship. Based on the evaluation results, the mentor and protégé will determine whether it is best to terminate the mentoring relationship. Let's face it: all relationships are not a match made in heaven. The mentor may determine their leadership style is not a good fit for the protégé. Contrarily, the protégé may feel the mentor's leadership style is not good for them. It may be you simply have outgrown one another. Whatever the reason, terminating a mentoring relationship does not have to be bad.

It is a wise decision to sever the relationship if key factors are misaligned. What do I mean? In the beginning, the mentor set the tone for the mentoring relationship. Both the mentor and the protégé expressed their expectations (or you should have). These expectations were the foundation for the mentoring relationship. If these expectations have not been met, it is safe to say that at this point they will continue to be ignored. It is wise to terminate the relationship. If the relationship lacks mutual respect, honesty, and direct communication, it may be time to terminate it. If neither the mentor nor protégé are committed to the relationship, it is time to terminate it. If the mentor and protégé no longer have shared values, trust, or are willing to work through challenges, it is time to terminate the relationship.

Ending a mentoring relationship, as previously stated, does not have to be negative. The mentor and protégé can sever the relationship and maintain a positive, friendly attitude. If the mentor feels they are unable to continue to mentor the protégé, be honest. I do not recommend saying, "Call me anytime" or making vague, open-ended statements. It is best to wish the protégé well by saying, "It has been a pleasure to serve you. I wish you well in your endeavors. Please keep me informed of your progress via email." This lets the protégé know the mentor cares about their future well-being.

If the protégé does not feel the mentor is a good fit, be honest as well. Provide positive feedback. Let the mentor know how they have benefited you. Start by saying, "Through this process, I have learned …" or "You have taught me …" By no means should the protégé feel guilty about separating from the mentor. If it is not a good fit or the protégé feels they have reached a plateau in the relationship, it is the protégé's decision to make. The protégé should be sure to be clear with the mentor about why they are ending the relationship. The protégé's feedback may assist the mentor in improving their leadership skills and abilities.

As the protégé, you are as much in control of the mentoring relationship as the mentor. Be honest about your observations and feelings about the progress of the relationship. If you do not feel the relationship is working, share this with your mentor.

Perhaps the mentor and protégé realize the mentoring relationship has crossed a particular boundary and is more personal. This is also a good reason to terminate the mentoring relationship. The mentor and protégé may decide to continue the relationship on a personal level as friends. This is not to say the mentor cannot be the protégé's friend; however, when the line crosses into a friendship, communication changes. Giving and receiving information is not done in the same manner. Your thoughts towards one another shift, and you become casual. It is easy to become too relaxed; thus, specific milestones and goals are overlooked. A lackadaisical approach to the relationship is taken, and what has been established is now on the back burner. Growth plateaus and can even come to a stop. The lines become blurred and it is difficult to ascertain the mentor from the protégé. I like what Ira Chaleff says,

> In the dance of leaders and followers, we change partners and roles throughout our lives ... If we are leading, we must lead; and if we are not, we must follow, but always as a strong partner. We constantly learn from each other and improve our gracefulness in a wide diversity of styles and tempos.[207]

Separation Anxiety

Depending upon how long the mentoring relationship was, the mentor or the protégé may experience a bit of separation anxiety. If it was a lengthy relationship,

---

[207] Ira Chaleff, *The Courageous Follower 3rd Edition* (San Francisco, CA: Berrett-Koehler Publishers, Inc.), 2009: 31.

the mentor and protégé grew attached to one another. Getting back to "normalcy" may not be easy as what was normal prior to the mentoring relationship is no longer normal. The mentor and protégé adapted their lives based on the relationship. The protégé became accustomed to the mentor's style of leadership. The mentor became accustomed to the protégé's learning curve. Both the mentor and protégé are accustomed to patterns of behavior, attitudes, and perceptions.

At the root of separation anxiety is fear and worry. In 2 Timothy 1:7, we are told God does not give us a spirit of fear, but one of power, love and sound judgment. Other versions use the term "sound mind" or "discipline". In the Greek, the word for discipline is sōphronismou (so-fron-os-mos'), or self-control. One thing about separation anxiety, according to WebMD, is the individual often has *unrealistic* thoughts that something bad will happen. To conquer this issue, the person must be willing to adjust their thoughts. If the protégé thinks bad things will happen to them or the mentor because of the relationship ending, the protégé should pray about changing their thoughts. The Bible declares in Proverbs 23:7a, "As he thinks in his heart, so is he."[208] When a person changes how they think about what is next in their life after the relationship, the fear and worry they have will disappear.

Separation anxiety does not have to be negative. It actually builds resiliency. When a person has a sense of belonging, a sense of worth and acceptance, and an understanding of their personal strengths and limitations, they are better able to overcome adversity. Thus, security, good self-esteem and a sense of self-efficacy build resiliency.[209] Highly resilient people can take an adverse situation and make it work to their advantage. They refuse to be victims. When a person plays the victim, they will not take steps to overcome the adversity. What happens is they proverbially handicap themselves. They begin to feel helpless and play the blame game – placing the responsibility to make their life better on other people.[210] Al Siebert believes,

---

[208] New King James Version, NKJV
[209] Brigid Daniel, and Sally Wassell, *The Early Years: Assessing and Promoting Resilience in Vulnerable Children 1, Volume 1* (London, England: Jessica Kingsley Publishers), 2002: 13.
[210] Al Siebert, *The Resiliency Advantage: Master Change, Thrive Under Pressure, and Bounce Back from Setbacks* (ReadHowYouWant.com), 2009: 3.

> Resilient people don't wait for others to rescue them; they work through their feelings, set goals, work to reach their goals, and often emerge from the resiliency process with a better life than before. Later they say they are glad that their difficult situation happened.[211]

While dealing with building resiliency, take the time to solidify plans on what to do next.

Time to Shift

You have decided to terminate your mentoring relationship, and you may be unclear on what to do next. You know you need to do something different. Prior to terminating the relationship, you had an idea of what you wanted to do. This is the time where you solidify your plans on what to do next.

The mentor may need to take some time to reflect on the relationship and the protégé's feedback. What did you do well? What are some areas the protégé recommended you improve? What could you have done better? Use this time to develop a blueprint for what is next in your life. The mentor may hold off on accepting any new mentoring relationships. The mentor may want to work on self-

---
[211] Ibid, 39

development. Perhaps the mentor placed a few projects on hold, so they could focus their energies on helping their protégé. Now the mentor has the time to devote to them. Perhaps the mentor may want to take the feedback from their protégé and discuss it with their mentor. The mentor's mentor may have recommendations or resources on how the mentor can address the feedback to improve their leadership skills. John Maxwell believes the key to personal development is being more *growth* oriented than *goal* oriented.[212] He goes on to write,

> There is no downside to making growth your goal. If you keep learning, you will be better tomorrow than you are today, and that can do so many things for you. Competence is a key to credibility, and credibility is the key to influencing others. If people respect you, they will listen to you. President Abraham Lincoln said, "I don't think much of a man who is not wiser today than he was yesterday." By focusing on growth, you become wiser each day.[213]

The protégé also should reflect on any feedback shared with them. What worked well? What are some areas the mentor recommended you improve? What could you

---

[212] John C. Maxwell, *The 360° Leader: Developing Your Influence from Anywhere in the Organization* (Nashville, TN: Thomas Nelson), 2005: 151.

[213] IBID, 151

have done better? The protégé can also use this time to develop a blueprint for what is next in their life. Review the notes from the Premature Stage. What was your original intent for getting a mentor? Assess how you have grown since that time. Establish new goals. The protégé should position themselves to meet new people. Whatever the protégé decides to do, the protégé should not remain stagnate. MOVE. To quote Jim Rohn, "If you go to work on your goals, your goals will go to work on you. If you go to work on your plan, your plan will go to work on you. Whatever good things we build end up building us." Whether the mentor or the protégé, this is a perfect time to be still and seek The Lord for guidance. Remember, prayer *p*urposefully *r*eveals *a*lignment strategies for *y*ou in *e*very *r*eal situation.

The Rebuilding Stage

> *Once you achieve one goal, you should be looking forward to trying to build onto the next thing, and not just getting comfortable with what you're doing.*
> ~ LL Cool J

Earlier, I stated the mentoring relationship evolves. Evolution involves change and requires constant rebuilding. After deciding to continue the mentoring relationship, at this stage, the mentor and protégé proceed with any necessary adjustments. Here, new goals are created to build upon those previously generated. Any of the initial goals that have not been achieved are addressed as well as what avenues you are going to explore to ensure they are reached. A close examination of the notes from the Assessment Stage is critical to the Rebuilding Stage. Those notes will be your blueprints. In addition, you will need to pull in notes from the Premature and Infant Stages.

Once all of the documentation is gathered, the mentor and the protégé need to discuss what direction to take the relationship. Will the new goals be focused on professional aspirations or will they be more personal? What is the purpose of this next leg of the mentoring relationship? As the definition implies, the purpose of this stage is to make extensive repairs or important improvements. It does not mean the relationship is a complete failure. It merely allows room to change directions. It, also, opens the door to building a new relationship.

What happens when distance becomes a factor in the mentoring relationship? This certainly creates a new dimension by which the mentoring relationship must adjust. It is highly probable someone in the mentoring relationship may relocate. It is also highly probable that the mentoring relationship began long-distance. Regardless of when the distance entered the relationship, it must be addressed. I am addressing it here opposed to elsewhere in the book to give you an idea of how to rebuild the mentoring relationship due to factors that have entered the relationship. Thus, moving forward in this discussion, I will address rebuilding the mentoring relationship when distance becomes a factor later in the relationship opposed to it being a factor from the beginning.

Today, technology affords us the opportunity to connect with each other easily. One-to-one contact does not have to be literal. We can use Skype, FaceTime, or Google Hangouts for face-to-face meetings. When distance becomes a factor, new boundaries will have to be established. Some of the same boundaries established earlier in the relationship will likely be kept; however, some of those boundaries may have to be amended. Other boundaries may be introduced. One boundary that will have to be addressed is how you will communicate, how often, and when. Consider for a moment the issue of time zone differences. Clear, appropriate guidelines on *when* it is acceptable to communicate via telephone, for example, will have to be established. If it is 5:00 PM in California (PST), it is 8:00 PM in Miami (EST). If it is 4:00 PM in New York, it is 10:00 PM in Amsterdam. It is not likely you will have regular telephone or online conversations at 10:00 PM if you are in Amsterdam. While this may seem like a stretch, it is realistic for many people. Email may be the primary method of communication. However, you must be diligent when using email.

Why is this important? Breakdowns in communication are likely to occur. Body language or non-verbal cues cannot be read in an email. A person's tone cannot be determined from reading an email. Misunderstanding is likely to occur. A simple typing error or an offhand remark can alter the tone of the email completely. Emoticons can help with this; however, they can come across as unprofessional and inappropriate to different cultures. Cheerfulness is encouraged; however, keep humor to a minimum. I recommend you include specific time zone requirements for responding in your email. Place this in your signature preferably. If you are in Atlanta, for example, you may want to be clear that all responses are on Eastern Standard Time (EST). You may also want to include the Greenwich Mean Time (GMT) to your email so the person overseas will know the difference between your time zone and theirs. For instance, the GMT for Central Standard Time is -6. This varies depending upon location.

Another thing to remember when using email correspondence is basic rules of etiquette, or netiquette. You want to avoid using capital letters, exclamation points, or red fonts. This can denote shouting or anger. If you need to emphasize a word or point, use italics, an asterisk, or place it in brackets. Avoid using slang, jargon, or colloquialisms. These things mean something to you; however, they translate differently to other people. Be mindful of the length of your emails as well as attachments.

The key to a successful long-distance mentoring relationship is communication.

You want to be considerate of the other person's bandwidth and their mailbox. You do not want your one email to take up the entire space of their inbox, preventing other messages from getting to them. If you have a large file to send, ZIP the file or ask the person how they would like you to send it to them. Cloud services are perfect for this. Google Drive and DropBox are good for sharing large files. With these services, you can limit what the individuals can do with the files. For instance, with Google Drive you can determine whether the person can view the file or view and edit. Always proofread your email before sending it. Run a spell and grammar check, because these things matter. Remember, emails are not private.

The key to a successful long-distance mentoring relationship is communication. If at all possible, I strongly recommend video-conferencing as often as possible. Skype is a free video-conferencing service that allows you to communicate by voice (using a microphone), by video (using a webcam), or by instant messaging (over the Internet). It is important to note that calls within the Skype service are free; calls to landline and mobile phones are not. Google Hangouts allows you to video chat with up to 10 people in one video call. However you choose to address distance in your mentoring relationship, make sure your boundaries are clear and your communication methods are clear as well.

Now that we have a deeper understanding of mentoring relationships, to include the roles of the mentor and protégé as well as the different stages of the mentoring relationship, we can expand our discussion. In the next chapter, we look at the relationship between mentoring and organizations. In reading the chapter, think about why mentoring is important to you as an individual. Then consider your own organization or an organization with which you are affiliated. Will a mentoring program be beneficial to the organization? Is it feasible? How can it improve leadership development? Let us continue ...

Mentoring and Organizations

> *An organization, no matter how well designed, is only as good as the people who live and work in it. ~ Dee Hock*

Today's 21st century organization relies heavily on the knowledge and creativity of their workforce as organizations from the past – specifically the Industrial era -- relied on the physical strengths of its labor force. Regardless of the era, people drive results. Thus, organizations must realize that the more they invest in their people, the more productivity increases resulting in higher profits. Laurie Bassie and Daniel McMurrer showed in a 2007 study in the Harvard Business Review that companies with high scores for their investments in human capital delivered stock market returns that were five times higher than that of companies with less emphasis on human capital.[214]

---

[214]"Driving Performance: Why Leadership Development Matters In Difficult Times," [PDF document], *Center for Creative*

Mentoring is a leadership development tool organizations can use to maximize performance. With it, organizations can strategically organize how they operate by focusing on the knowledge capacity of its environment.

> Mentorship aids in the development of managerial talent for the organization. Not only do these relationships help young professionals learn technical knowledge, but they also aid them in learning the organizational ropes, developing a sense of competence and effectiveness, and learning how to behave at successive management levels.[215]

When an organization adopts a formal mentoring program, the mentoring program should adapt as the organization evolves. Mentoring provides a structured system for strengthening and assuring the continuity of organizational culture.[216] One that provides members with a common value

Today's organization is more about intellectual capital and less about physical labor.

Leadership, 2008, http://www.ccl.org/leadership/pdf/landing/DrivingPerformance.pdf

[215] David Marshall Hunt, and Carol Michael, "Mentorship: A Career Training and Development Tool," *Academy of Management Review* 8, 1983: 475-485.

[216] James A. Wilson, and Nancy S. Elman, "Organizational benefits of mentoring," *The Executive* 4, no. 4, 1990: 88-94.

base with implicit knowledge of what is expected of them and what they, in turn, can expect from the organization; this can be vital to organizational success and effectiveness.[217]

Some mentoring relationships become more than about improving the individual one-dimensionally. The mentor looks at how they can help the person holistically. Part of mentoring is getting the person to understand who they are: This takes into account the person's social identity as well as their cultural beliefs and values. When the mentoring relationship is associated with the work environment, this level of development is equally as important. From an employee perspective, when they feel their manager has a concern for their personal well-being, their level of trust increases. When an employee's trust level increases, their commitment to the organization solidifies. They look beyond the monetary value of their job and look at the social relationships, purpose and cultural-fit which results in reduced turnover.[218] In terms of volunteer

---

[217] Ibid

[218] Jeffrey Pfeffer, "Working Alone: Whatever Happened to the Idea of Organizations as Communities?" In James O'Toole and Edward E. Lawler (1st ed), *The New American Workplace* (New York, NY: Palgrave MacMillan), 2005: 133-138.

organizations, like a church (localized assembly of believers), the same principle applies. When members of the church volunteer their time and talent to advance the work of the church, they do so because they are committed to the mission and vision of that church. Trust has been established. Belief expanded. They have an interest in the well-being of the church and, consequently, the communities the church affects.

Another potential benefit of mentoring relationships in organizations is reduced turnover. Through the mentoring program, there is a greater pool of qualified internal applicants to promote from within the organization. This reduces employee stress over job stability and increases morale. It also helps with succession planning. In succession planning, the goal is to recruit those employees who are superior in their performance. These employees are coachable as well. They are open to improving their knowledge, skills, and abilities in order to advance to a higher role within the organization.

As the organization takes a stake in the lives of the people, the people unify and their behavior towards one another is civil. This leads to reduced instances of workplace bullying and harassment, which in recent years have led to instances of turnover and even suicide. In a 2012 Workplace Bullying Institute survey, 29% of bullied targets stated they considered suicide and 16% actually had a plan to execute it. In 2013, a California teacher committed suicide after her school principal and assistant principal reportedly belittled her in front of teachers and students. Reportedly, she was assigned to teach a class she was not knowledgeable about; however, if she refused to teach the class she would not have been granted the opportunity to teach the class she wanted. After enduring the abuse,

> She took stress leave, receiving half her salary for a short time. Her claims for disability insurance and workers' compensation were both denied. She took out a personal loan to live. The district gave her two options: resign or apply for a waiting list for rehire. She was at the end of her rope. Her mother had given her rent money. The next day, July 1, she took her life.[219]

---

[219] "Another Teacher Suicide With Workplace Bullying Causal Factors," *Workplace Bullying Institute* September 11, 2013, http://www.workplacebullying.org/2013/09/11/lenihan/

As previously stated, mentoring is a leadership development tool. When the organization pairs employees with leaders to develop future leaders, they create a culture that says to the employees, "We care about you. We see your potential and want to cultivate that so you can achieve the goals and aspirations you have set for yourself. And if you have not set these for yourself, we want to push you so you can advance anyway." This is not only the case for leaders developing employees; this can be the case for leaders improving their own leadership skills as well. Am I saying leaders can be their own mentors? Absolutely!

Mentoring is a leadership development tool to which every organization (for profit and non-profit) should consider allocating resources. The long-term benefits exceed the initial investment.

When companies invest in the development of their people, the return can be enormous. When the US Postal Service collaborated with the Center for Creative Leadership to invest in leadership development, they saw a cumulative cost savings of $8.8 billion.[220] While it may take

---

[220] "Driving Performance: Why Leadership Development

upwards of three years to see the full result or impact of the investment, Aaron Kraus and Chantale Wilson share,

> One study assessing successful organizations that were actively engaged in leadership development found the average investment in those activities was 500,000 and the average ROI was $1 million. Returns manifested in improved global competitiveness, profitability, sales, and shareholder value, which illustrates the extensive benefits and potential spillover effect of investing in leadership development.[221]

When Christian leaders develop themselves and others, it is important for them to be willing to elevate their consciousness of the world around them, the applicable methods and principles, and uncover any innovation that exists to help them establish (or re-establish) basic Biblical principles in modern times on a global scale. This may be challenging, especially if the Christian leader is working in a non-Christian organization. Regardless of the work environment, the leader must see themselves as their own mentor before being a mentor to others. What does this

---

Matters In Difficult Times" [PDF document], *Center for Creative Leadership*, 2008, http://www.ccl.org/leadership/pdf/landing/DrivingPerformance.pdf

[221] Aaron J. Kraus, and Chantale N. Wilson, "Leadership development for organizational success" [PDF document], *Society for Industrial and Organizational Psychology, Inc.*, 2012

mean? A leader must have a sense of their ability to think and learn. Learning is a process of self-change that involves leaders exposing themselves to new paths they would not normally follow.[222] What does this entail?

> The leadership journey requires an honest assessment of one's life and abilities. It requires continuous learning, a love of knowledge, and the desire to embrace the changes that will occur. It will require stamina, perseverance and tenacity as it is not a short trip with an end in sight. True leadership is an on-going education of life-long and continuous learning.[223]

Mentoring and Diversity Management

When it comes to diversity, it is important to realize it is more than a buzzword. Diversity is a common element in the 21st century, particularly in organizations. Diversity

---

[222] Mette Vestergaard, "The Leader Is His Own Mentor: Commentary with Mette Vestergaard," *Emerald Group Publishing Limited*, www.emeraldinsight.com.library.regent.edu/learning/management_thinking/articles/leader_mentor.htm

[223] Diane J. Hollo, "The Role of Mentorship in Leadership Development and Career Success," (Unpublished dissertation, Carroll University, Waukesha, Wisconsin), May 2011: 37.

affects the way people interact with one another, both as individuals and collectively.

> For successful business, diversity is much more than a buzzword or the 'right thing to do'. In thriving companies across the globe, diversity is an essential tool that creates a competitive. Diversity brings thoughts, feelings and cultural knowledge that can benefit operations, decision making, marketing, culture-building, hiring, firing and just about everything that a business does.[224]

Daft examines diversity as both basic dimensions and secondary dimensions.[225] Basic dimensions are things such as race, ethnicity, or gender. These are differences embedded in an individual's DNA and will influence them throughout their life. As such, they have the propensity to shape the individual's perspectives or their self-images. Secondary dimensions are those things the individual learn and can be changed.

Milliken and Martin believe diversity is a double-edged sword.[226] They believe it increases the opportunity

---

[224] Vidhi Agrawal, ("Managing the Diversified Team: Challenges and Strategies for Improving Performance," *Team Performance Management* 18, no. 7/8, 2012: 387, doi: 10.1108/13527591211281129

[225] Richard L. Daft, *Management 6th Edition* (London: Thomson Learning), 2003.

for creativity while at the same time increases the likelihood of dissatisfaction and failure to identify with one's workgroup.[227] This may have everything to do with the difference between cultures and how individuals react/respond to certain situations. Emotional responses are not uncommon; therefore, leaders must be able to effectively address such responses while managing diversity.

With respect to managing diversity in the workplace, Ayoko and Hartel believe managers and group leaders need to have the ability to recognize emotional processes in their workgroups to promote positive emotional processes and manage negative emotional processes for positive outcomes.[228] They go on to say, "Given that leadership is often credited with successful performance in international competition, it is important to secure leaders who can effectively manage culturally diverse workgroups."[229]

---

[226] Frances J. Milliken, and Luis L. Martins, "Searching for Common Threads: Understanding the Multiple Effects of Diversity in Organizational Groups" *Academy of Management Review* 21, 1996: 402-433.
[227] Ibid
[228] Oluremi B. Ayoko, and Charmine E.J. Hartel, "The Role Of Emotion And Emotion Management In Destructive And Productive Conflict In Culturally Heterogeneous Workgroups" In Neal M. Ashkanasy, Charmine E.J. Hartel, and W.J. Zerbe, *Managing Emotions In The Workplace,* (New York, NY: M.E. Sharpe, Armonk), 2002.

With the overlap of cultures across borders and oceans as well as advances in technology, organizations and societies are more culturally diverse than in the past. Depending on the job classification, employees are able to work remotely while simultaneously coming together for a common goal. With the use of Skype, OoVoo, Adobe Connect, Join Me, and Go to Meeting – for example - people in India can communicate with people in the United Kingdom, the United States, or parts of Asia on a project that, in years past, may have been difficult to complete. Technological advances highlight the dynamics of the global workforce as well as the global community and sheds light on the value of diversity. It, also, places a spotlight on why organizational leaders must have a firm understanding of diversity in order to maximize the potential of their diversified workforce. Businesses today need to understand better other cultures and varied ages, genders, and lifestyles.

The 21st century organization is a multi-cultural, multi-dimensional organism composed of people from all walks of life. They are comprised of people from high-

---

[229] Ibid, 351

context cultures, low-context cultures, individualistic cultures as well as collectivist cultures. With all of these factors, and so many more, organizations have discovered the need to integrate diversity into their strategic business plans. Many of them now have strategic plans that address short-term and long-term diversity challenges as well as accountability measures for managers working with cross-cultural and inter-cultural teams. Lockwood argues,

> Workplace diversity is no longer only about anti-discrimination compliance. It now focuses on both inclusion and the impact on the company's bottom line. Leveraging workplace diversity is now seen as a critical strategic resource for establishing a competitive advantage. Companies are beginning to link workplace diversity to both their long-range and immediate strategic goals and objectives and they are holding management accountable for the results.[230]

The roots of diversity management trace back as early as the 1950s in the United States when the issue of Affirmative Action and Civil Rights for African Americans was a hot topic. But, specifically, what is diversity management? Diversity management, while based on

---

[230] Nancy R. Lockwood, "Workplace Diversity: Leveraging the Power Of Difference For Competitive Advantage," *Society of Human Resource Management*, 2005, www.shrm.org/research/quarterly/2005/0605RQuart_essay.asp#f8#f8

cultural change, is a pragmatic business strategy that focuses on maximizing the productivity, creativity, and commitment of the workforce, while meeting the needs of diverse consumer groups.[231] According to Fleury, cultural diversity management is an organizational answer or reaction to the need for competitiveness and to the increasing variety of the workforce.[232]

Culturally diverse teams provide an efficient, flexible way to maximize productivity through the use of the skills, talents, and information of the collective team.

What can a culturally diverse workforce do for an organization? Literature is full of explanations; however, I will only share a few. Diverse teams can boost performance, because they are more likely to have access to the breadth of information necessary to solve complex problems.[233]

---

[231] "Managing a multicultural workforce", *Black Enterprise* 7, 2001: 120.

[232] Maria Tereza Leme Fleury, "The Management of Culture Diversity: Lessons from Brazilian Companies," *Industrial Management and Data Systems* 99, no. 3, 1999: 109-114.

[233] Jonathan S. Leonard, David I. Levine, and Aparna Joshi, "Do Birds of a Feather Shop Together? The Effects on Performance of Employees' Similarity with One Another and With Customers," *Journal of Organizational Behavior* 25, no. 6, 2004: 731-54.

Opinions of a culturally diverse workforce can lead to higher quality decisions.[234, 235] Companies that incorporate employees' diverse perspectives to rethink primary tasks and redefine markets, products, strategies, missions, business practices, and even cultures are tapping diversity's true benefits by making more creative and better decisions.[236, 237] Today's organization is more about intellectual capital and less about physical labor. Intellect crosses all colors, backgrounds, genders, and orientations. Culturally diverse teams provide an efficient, flexible way to maximize productivity through the use of the skills, talents, and information of the collective team.

The challenge of managing diversity in practice is in dealing appropriately with the goals of the organization

---

[234] Taylor Cox, Jr. *Cultural Diversity In Organizations: Theory, Research, And Practice* (San Francisco, CA: Berrett-Koehler Publishers), 1994

[235] Poppy Lauretta McLeod, Sharon Alisa Lobel, and Taylor H. Cox, Jr., "Ethnic Diversity and Creativity in Small Groups," *Small Group Research* 27, no. 2, 1996: 246-264.

[236] Susan E. Jackson, "Consequences of Group Composition for the Interpersonal Dynamics of Strategic Issue Processing," In Paul Shrivastava, Anne Huff, and Jane Dutton, *Advances In Strategic Management* (Greenwich, CT: JAI Press), 1992: 345-385.

[237] David A. Thomas, and Robin J. Ely, "Making Differences Matter," *Harvard Business Review* 74, no. 5, 1996: 79-90.

versus the needs of individuals and harmonizing the two sets of requirements.[238] Where there is high diversity, teams enter into debate due to their different perceptions of the strategic environment and the range of possible strategic options. Rather than accepting existing strategies and routine ways of operating, diverse teams are liable to engage in conflict, fueled by their different perspectives.[239] Management's role is to help create and empower an organizational culture that fosters a respectful, inclusive, knowledge-based environment where each employee has the opportunity to learn, grow and meaningfully contribute to the organization's success.[240]

As organizations grow and expand in the global marketplace, they will need leaders who are ready to advance and hone their skills. When organizations expand

---

[238] Latanya Hughes. "The Borderless Organization," (Unpublished paper, Regent University, Virginia Beach, VA), 2013.

[239] Vidhi Agrawal, "Managing The Diversified Team: Challenges And Strategies For Improving Performance," *Team Performance Management* 18, no. 7/8, 2012: 389, DOI: 10.1108/13527591211281129

[240] Nancy R. Lockwood, "Workplace Diversity: Leveraging The Power Of Difference For Competitive Advantage," *Society for Human Resource Management,* 2005, www.shrm.org/research/quarterly/2005/0605RQuart_essay.asp#f8#f8

into other markets, cross-cultural adaptation is necessary for the leader. According to Black, Morrison and Gregersen, a leader's personal character forges a critical dimension of global leadership.[241] "Your strong personal character sets an example within the company and creates a working environment that supports your implementation."[242] Expatriates often find themselves challenged when on foreign soil. The use of a mentor would greatly benefit the leader. When people immerse themselves into a foreign culture, their entire being is affected. How so? Expatriates are affected psychologically as well as socially. This can cause depression, anxiety, tension, and fatigue. Ward and Kennedy believe these attributes affect the expatriate's ability to negotiate interactive aspects of the host culture as measured by the amount of difficulty experienced in the management of everyday situations in the host culture.[243]

---

[241] J. Stewart Black, Allen J. Morrison, and Hal B. Gregersen, *Global Explorers: The Next Generation of Leaders* (New York: Routledge), 1999: 111.

[242] IBID

[243] Colleen Ward, and Antony Kennedy, "Crossing Cultures: The Relationship Between Psychological And Socio-Cultural Dimensions Of Cross-Cultural Adjustment," In Janak Pandey, Durganand Sinha and Dharm P.S. Bhawuk (Eds.), *Asian Contributions To Cross-Cultural Psychology*, (New Delhi: Sage Publications), 1996.

This can have a negative effect on their ability to perform. In this capacity, the leader faces the challenge of how to lead in a diverse climate. The leader can read countless literature on Geert Hofstede's Cultural Framework or Edward T. Hall's work on culture. However beneficial these theoretical frameworks are, the leader will need someone to guide them through the practical applications of day-to-day life in the respective culture in which they find themselves immersed. This is especially the case if it is their first expatriate experience.

> A first time expatriate is uninformed about his or her reactions to and ability to live in another country. Depending on the length of stay, the expatriate will or will not be able to reach a relatively stable state in the foreign location. After a few months, most people will have learned enough about their own reactions to cross-cultural moves to make a subsequent move significantly less novel as they can anticipate their reactions and feelings. For previous experience to become an adaptation facilitating force, although, it must have been a positive one.[244]

In this environment, the leader can potentially sharpen their diversity management skills. This, in turn,

---

[244] Arno Haslberger, "Facets And Dimensions Of Cross-Cultural Adaptation: Refining The Tools," *Personnel Review* 34, no. 1, 2005: 85-109, doi: 10.1108/00483480510571897

helps improve diversity management within the organization. As the leader immerses in the culture and "learns the ropes," they apply what they have learned by integrating it with their leadership skills. Employees see this effort; their respect and trust for the leader and the organization increases, resulting in an increase in employee motivation, morale, and productivity.

What's Next?

> *I am personally convinced that one person can be a change catalyst, a transformer in any situation, any organization. Such an individual is yeast that can leaven an entire loaf. It requires vision, initiative, patience, respect, persistence, courage, and faith to be a transforming leader.* ~ Stephen Covey

The mentoring relationship is a dynamic one that involves a delicate balance of nurturing and support on the one hand with stretch and challenge on the other. When it comes to mentoring, people must be willing to ask a few questions.

- Do people really want to be mentored?
- Are they serious about being mentored?
- Are they willing to pay for it – individually or as an organization?
- Do people feel mentoring is worth their time and effort to be mentored?
- Does leadership believe mentoring is necessary?

These questions force the mentor and the protégé to consider the costs of the relationship. This includes what the protégé wants, what the mentor requires as well as the sacrifice and the submission.

At each stage of the mentoring relationship, it is critical for the mentor to take notes. Lack of proper note taking can cause the mentor to lose focus in the relationship. Keep a journal of the protégé's progress. Ask questions. Are they on track? Take notes on what you are observing, conversations, feedback you get from their employer, family, friends, etc. Where do you begin? Here are a few questions to ask:

1. How do they see things, i.e. their perspective on their world?
2. What do they believe in or what is important to them?
3. What is their attitude or outlook toward the people and setting around them?
4. What is their view and pattern of thinking?

These questions the mentor can ponder throughout the duration of the mentoring relationship. This information is vital to the success of the mentoring relationship. Without this information, the mentor will not be able to assess the effectiveness of the relationship when reaching the Assessment Stage. This requires the mentor to be organized and focused. Remember, Jesus was organized. A disorganized and unfocused mentor can hinder the success of the relationship. If the mentor is disorganized and unfocused, how effective can they be at helping their protégé?

The mentor must be honest. If the mentor lacks knowledge in a particular area the protégé specifically needs help with and is dishonest about it, this can hinder the relationship. The protégé may take note of this and may decide to terminate the relationship. The protégé may also decide to terminate the mentoring relationship if they feel the mentor's style is not conducive for the mentoring relationship to flourish.

The mentoring relationship is a dynamic one that involves a delicate balance of nurturing and support on the one hand with stretch and challenge on the other.

There will be growing pains in the relationship. Both the mentor and protégé must be willing to work through those growing pains. In the event the two are unable to work through the growing pains after 3-6 months, it may be wise to terminate the relationship. In the event the mentor finds there is someone else who may be a better fit for the protégé, the mentor should speak with the recommended individual *before* mentioning him or her to the protégé. What happens if you recommend the individual to the protégé and that individual is unavailable or does not agree to mentor the protégé? The mentor does not want the protégé to feel as if they are being given the run around or as if they are bothersome to the mentor. The transition to a new mentor needs to be smooth (or as smooth as possible) so the protégé can have a positive attitude and disposition about the change. Moreover, the protégé needs to feel comfortable with the recommendation.

Proper follow-up is necessary when handing the protégé off to someone else. What if the recommendation turns out not to be a good fit? If it is a disjointed connection and there is no follow-up, the protégé may feel as if the mentor did not have an interest in them from the beginning. If the transition is occurring within an organization, once the new relationship has formed, it is necessary for human resources to maintain communication with the mentors (old and new) and the protégé. The feedback is vital to the success of the organization's mentoring program. It will help human resources match candidates with other leaders as the program advances.

Human resources must also take detailed notes (as detailed as possible) in order to properly evaluate the success of the mentoring relationships and the mentoring program. Frequent discussions between human resources and the mentors and protégés (collectively and individually) should take place. The goal is to gather candid feedback. In these sessions, human resources can gage the health of the program as well as see if their matching techniques are accurate. They can also use the candid feedback to see how vested the individuals are. Are they going through the motions or really interacting? They will also ascertain how much support the program gets from high-ranking company officials. Are the high-ranking company officials vested in the mentoring program? Reports will need to show measurable data (return on investment) at some point. Initially changes will be small, depending on

Culture is a sensitive subject and must be handled with care when establishing a corporate mentoring program.

the protégé. Others may be instant. Motivation is definitely a factor.

When establishing a corporate mentoring program, human resources must consider the culture of the organization and the individuals involved. For example, women differ from men. Ethnic cultures and differences between generations must be considered as well. It will also be necessary to address the key players, establish the commitment, have strategic conversations, and examine person-org fit. Interviews will have to be conducted. The interview questions should be tailored to the people you are interview, i.e. the mentor and the protégé. What does mentoring mean to them? Why is it important? What is the impact to them and the organization? You want to use discovery questions.[245] In this process, be like a journalist: who, what, when, where, how, and why. One question should lead to another question. How will a mentoring program advance or grow the organization? How will it

---

[245] Peter Block, *Flawless Consulting: A Guide to Getting Your Expertise Used 2nd Edition*, (San Francisco, CA: Jossey-Bas/Pfeiffer), 2000: 189-206.

affect the company's culture? What affect will it have on innovation?

From an organizational perspective, you do have to consider the cost to the company as well as the cost to the person doing the mentoring (specifically in allotted time). Is it worth the time and effort to invest in a mentoring program? What is the expected return on investment? If the organization decides to implement a mentoring program, how will scheduling be addressed for both mentor and protégé? How long, in terms of cycle, will the mentoring session last?

You will need to address limitations to a company mentoring program. These limitations may include lack of support for the program. This may be in the form of availability, time, or available financial resources. You may not have enough qualified applicants or candidates or not enough mentors creating an unbalanced ratio. You may have a problem matching or mismatching mentors to protégés.

Whether individual or organizational, when you enter a mentoring relationship, you are accepting responsibility for this person. The mentor becomes the protégé's trusted advisor. Please do not think for one moment that this is going to happen overnight. "The fact is trust does not happen without work, without volition, and without effort."[246] It is a two-way street. There are things that can be done to prove trustworthiness, but the mentor must realize they cannot do this on their own. The protégé must participate and reciprocate. The fact this person sought the mentor out is a start. It shows on some level that they trust the mentor's leadership abilities or what they have heard about the mentor's leadership abilities. Hughes and Beatty believe,

The mentor must remember they are a trusted advisor to the protégé. To violate this trust goes against the principles of Christian mentoring and any mentoring relationship.

> By allowing themselves to be influenced, they are changing their beliefs, attitudes, and behaviors in ways that you request. They must trust your competence, your motivations, your style; and they must trust that you are going to take them to a place that is better than where they are today.[247]

---

[246] David H. Maister, Charles H. Green, and Robert M. Galford, *The Trusted Advisor* (New York, NY: Free Press), 2000.

[247] Richard L. Hughes, and Katherine C. Beatty, *Becoming A Strategic Leader: Your Role In Your Organization's Enduring Success* (San

Christian mentors are developing different sides of their protégé much like a Rubix Cube. On one side, the mentor is creating a change agent. On another, they are teaching them to be revolutionary. On yet another side, the mentor is teaching the protégé to challenge the status quo, if necessary, by taking the road less traveled. Still, the mentor is self-empowering the protégé. The mentor is teaching the protégé to have an open mind. The mentor teaches the protégé to be willing to abandon pre-conceived notions. Finally, the mentor develops the protégé to be knowledge storehouses.

Think about Christian mentoring in terms of braiding. To make a braid, you need three pieces of the material (hair or rope). In a Christian mentoring relationship, the three pieces weaving together to form the braid are Jesus, the mentor, and the protégé. The mentor and the protégé intertwine as they both intertwine around Jesus. "A rope made from three strands of cord is hard to break."[248]

Francisco, CA: Jossey-Bass), 2005.
[248] Ecclesiastes 4:12b (Contemporary English Version, CEV)

Glossary

Affiliative leaders - create people connections and harmony within the organization; focuses on emotional needs over work needs.

Agape love – selfless, unconditional love

Agapao (ag-ap-ah'-o) – how people show love to one another.

Autocratic leadership - a leader who makes decisions without consulting with others.

Baby Boomers – people born during the Post-World War II baby boom between 1946 and 1964.

Benevolent authoritative leaders - add concern for people to an authoritative position; uses rewards to encourage appropriate performance and listens more to concerns lower down the organization.

Commanding leaders - give clear directions by his or her powerful stance, commanding and expecting full compliance

Coaching - partnering with clients in a thought-provoking and creative process that inspires them to maximize their personal and professional potential.

Coaching leaders - connect wants to organizational goals; help people find strengths and weaknesses and tie them to career aspirations and actions.

Consultative leadership - the leader makes an effort to listen carefully to ideas.

Democratic leader - acts to value inputs and commitment via participation, listening to both the bad and the good news. Finally, commanding leaders give clear directions by his or her powerful stance, commanding and expecting full compliance.

Democratic leadership - involves the people in the decision-making; however, the process for the final decision may vary from the leader having the final say to them facilitating consensus in the group.

Didaskalos (did-as'-kal-os) – (Greek) one who is fitted to teach.

Eros love – passionate, intense, intimate love

Exagorazo (ex-ag-or-ad'-zo) – (Greek) to buy up, i.e. ransom, to rescue from loss (improve opportunity).

Exploitive authoritative leaders - have a low concern for people and use such methods as threats and other fear-based methods to achieve conformance.

Generation X (GenX) – people born after the Western Post World War II baby boom between 1965 and 1980.

Hofstede's Cultural Dimensions – a framework for cross-cultural communication.

Kairos (kahee-ros') – (Greek) an occasion, i.e. set or proper time – always, opportunity, (convenient, due) season, (due, short, while) time, a while.

Kasha (kaw-saw') – (Hebrew) cover.

Laissez-faire leadership - minimizes the leader's involvement and allows people to make their own decisions, although the leader may still be responsible for the outcome.

Mentor - someone who teaches or gives help and advice to a less experienced and often younger person; a trusted counselor or guide.

Microexpressions – brief, involuntary, emotionally-driven facial expressions.

Millenials (GenY or Generation Y) – a person reaching young adulthood around the year 2000.

Milestone - marks a significant change or stage in development.

Monochronic or "M" time – individuals who are "sticklers" for time; everything operates and functions according to a schedule.

Pace-setting leaders - build challenge and exciting goals for people, expecting excellence and often exemplifying it themselves.

Parakletos (par-ak'-lay-tos) – (Greek) to counsel, assist, advise, or support.

Participative leaders - people lower down the organization so people across the organization are psychologically closer and work well together at all levels.

Phileo love – brotherly love.

PILLAR – term used to define the stages of the mentoring relationship (Premature, Infant, Learning, Living, Assessment, and Rebuilding).

PLUS - an acronym for Prayer, Listening, Understanding, and Servant; critical attributes Christian leaders must develop when mentoring others.

Polychronic individuals - prefer a higher degree of liberty; always multiple things happening at once.

Protégé - someone who has agreed to submit to the authority of a mentor with the intent to learn and grow from them.

Servant leadership - a leader's desire to motivate and guide followers, offer hope, and provide a more caring experience through established quality relationships

Situational leadership - responding to situations.

SMART - specific, measurable, attainable, realistic, and timely

Sōphronismou (so-fron-os-mos') – (Greek) discipline or self-control

Transactional leadership - the leader exchanges things of value with their followers to advance their own and their follower's agendas.

Transformational leadership - leaders make followers into self-empowered leaders and into change agents.

Values - those realities people believe in at the deepest level, so much so that they dictate people's decisions and their leadership

Visionary leaders - move people toward a shared vision, telling them where to go.

Ya'ats (yaw-ats) – (Hebrew) it means to advise, consult, give counsel, counsel, purpose, devise, or plan.

Yadah (yaw-daw') – (Hebrew) to know, to cause to know, to teach.

Yā-rūs (yaw-rutz) – (Hebrew) to run (for whatever reason, especially to rush) - to break down, divide speedily, footman, guard, bring hastily, (make) run (away, through), post.

Bibliography

Adler, Nancy J. "Communicating Across Cultural Barriers." *International Dimensions of Organizational Behavior* (2nd ed.). Boston, MA: PWS-KENT Publishing Company, 1991.

"African cultural values." Accessed June 2, 2012, http://www.emeka.at/african_cultural_vaules.pdf

Agrawal, Vidhi. (2012). "Managing The Diversified Team: Challenges And Strategies For Improving Performance." *Team Performance Management* 18, no. 7/8 (2012): 384-400. doi: 10.1108/13527591211281129

"Another Teacher Suicide with Workplace Bullying Causal Factors." *Workplace Bullying Institute*, September 11, 2013, http://www.workplacebullying.org/2013/09/11/lenihan/

Ayoko, Oluremi B. and Hartel, Charmine E.J. "The Role of Emotion and Emotion Management in Destructive and Productive Conflict in Culturally Heterogeneous Workgroups." In Neal M. Ashkanasy, Charmine E.J. Hartel, and W.J. Zerbe, *Managing Emotions in the Workplace.* New York, NY: M.E. Sharpe, Armonk, 2002.

Ayoko, Oluremi B. and Hartel, Charmine E.J. "Cultural Diversity and Leadership: A Conceptual Model of Leader Intervention in Conflict Events in Culturally

Heterogeneous Workgroups." *Cross Cultural Management: An International Journal* 13, no. 4, 2006: 345-360. doi: 10.1108/13527600610713431

Barbato, Patricia. *Inspire Your Career: Strategies for Success in Your First Years at Work*. Ontario, Canada: Insomniac Press, 2010.

Bass, Bernard M. *Leadership and Performance Beyond Expectations.* New York, NY: The Free Press, 1985.

Bekker, Corné, Ph.D. (2012). "The Origin of Value." Presentation at Regent University School of Leadership Residency, Virginia Beach, VA, May 7-12, 2012.

Bekker, Corné, Ph.D. (2012). "Mimetic Leadership." Presentation at Regent University School of Leadership Residency, Virginia Beach, VA, May 7-12, 2012.

Bell, Chip R. M*anagers as Mentors: Building Partnerships for Learning* (2nd edition). San Francisco, CA: Berrett-Koehler Publishers, Inc., 2002.

Bennis, Warren and Nanus, Burt. *Leaders: Strategies for Taking Charge*. New York: Collins Business, 2007.

Bjerregaard, Toke, Lauring, Jakob and Klitmoller, Anders. "A critical analysis of intercultural communication research in cross-cultural management: Introducing newer developments in anthropology." *Critical*

Perspectives on International Business 5, no. 3, 2009: 207-228. doi: 10.1108/17422040910974695

Black, J, Stewart, Morrison, Allen and Gregersen, Hal. *Global Explorers: The Next Generation of Leaders.* New York, NY: Routledge, 1999.

Block, Peter. *Flawless Consulting: A Guide to Getting Your Expertise Used* (2nd Edition). San Francisco, CA: Jossey-Bas/Pfeiffer, 2000.

Boorstein, Michelle. "Some Nonbelievers Still Find Solace in Prayer." *The Washington Post,* June 24, 2013, http://www.washingtonpost.com/local/non-believers-say-their-prayers-to-no-one/2013/06/24/b7c8cf50-d915-11e2-a9f2-42ee3912ae0e_story.html

Boros, Smaranda, Meslec, Nicoleta, Curseu, Petru L. and Emons, Wilco. "Struggles for Cooperation: Conflict Resolution Strategies in Multicultural Groups." *Journal of Managerial Psychology* 25, no. 5, 2010: 539-554. doi: 10.1108/02683941011048418

Braham, Jim. "The spiritual side." *Industry Week* 248, no. 3, 1999: 48-56.

Brennan, Richard. *Change Your Posture, Change Your Life: How the Power of the Alexander Technique Can Combat Back Pain, Tension and Stress.* London, UK: Duncan Baird Publishers, 2012.

Briner, Bob and Pritchard, Ray. *The Leadership Lessons of Jesus*. Nashville, TN: Broadman and Holman Publishers, 1997.

Cartwright, Mark. "Column." *Encyclopedia: Ancient History*, 2012, http://www.ancient.eu.com/column/

Chaleff, Ira. *The Courageous Follower* (3rd ed). San Francisco, CA: Berrett-Koehler Publishers, Inc., 2009.

Chong, Eric and Wolf, Helene. "Factors Influencing Followers' Perception of Organizational Leaders." *Leadership and Organization Development Journal* 31, no. 5, 2010: 402-419. doi: 10.1108/01437731011056434.

Colker, Jay O. *A Grounded Theory Approach to Developing a Theory of Leadership through a Case Study of ShoreBank*. Doctoral dissertation, University of Phoenix, 2008.

"Comprehensive needs assessment." *United States Department of Education*, 2001, http://www2.ed.gov/admins/lead/account/compneedsassessment.pdf

Covey, Stephen. R. *The Speed of Trust: The One Thing That Changes Everything*. New York, NY: Free Press, 2006.

Cox, Elaine, Bachkirova, Tatiana, and Clutterbuck, David. *The Complete Handbook of Coaching* (2nd ed). Sage Publication, 2014.

Cox, Jr. Taylor. *Cultural Diversity in Organizations: Theory, Research, and Practice.* San Francisco, CA: Berrett-Koehler Publishers, 1994.

Creswell, John W. *Research Design: Qualitative, Quantitative, and Mixed Methods Approaches 3rd Edition.* Los Angeles, CA: Sage Publications, 2009.

Daft, Richard L. *Theory and Design of Organizations* (10th ed.). Singapore: Cengage Learning, 2010.

Dalakoura, Afroditi. "Differentiating Leader and Leadership development: A Collective Framework for Leadership Development," *Journal of Management Development* 29, no. 5, 2010: 433 DOI:10.1108/02621711011039204

Daniel, Brigid and Wassell, Sally. *The Early Years: Assessing and Promoting Resilience in Vulnerable Children 1, Volume 1.* London, England: Jessica Kingsley Publishers, 2002: 13.

DeSilva, David A. *An Introduction to the New Testament: Contexts, Methods, and ministry Formation,* Downers Grove, IL: InterVarsity Press, 2004.

"Driving performance: Why leadership development matters in difficult times." *Center for Creative Leadership,* 2008, http://www.ccl.org/leadership/pdf/landing/DrivingPerformance.pdf

Edmondson, Amy. "Framing for Learning: Lessons in Successful Technology Implementation." *California Management Review* 45, no. 2, 2003: 34-54.

"Quichua Indians Ecuador." *El Jardin Aleman*, Accessed June 2, 2012, http://www.eljardinaleman.com/quichua_indians.htm

Ellwood, Robert S. and Alles, Gregory D. *Encyclopedia of World Religions*. Infobase Publishing, 2009.

Emelo, Randy. "Conversations with Mentoring Leaders." *ASTD*, July 2011: 36.

Erikson, Erik H. *Childhood and Society*. New York, NY: WW Horton and Company, Inc., 1950.

Evans, Matt H. "Course 18: Leadership." Accessed July 16, 2012, www.exinfm.com/training/pdfiles/course18.pdf

"Failed Bank Information: ShoreBank." *FDIC*, May 16, 2013, http://www.fdic.gov/bank/individual/failed/shorebank.html

Fleury, Maria Tereza Leme. "The Management of Culture Diversity: Lessons from Brazilian Companies." *Industrial Management and Data Systems* 99, no. 3, 1999: 109-114.

Foster, George, Davila, Antonio, Haemmig, Martin, He, Xiaobin, Jia, Ning, Bismark, Max von, and Wellman, Kerry. "Global Entrepreneurship and the Successful Growth Strategies of Early Stage Companies." *World Economic Forum*, 2011: 325.

Gladstone, Mia S. *Mentoring: A Strategy for Learning In A Rapidly Changing Society*. Montreal, Quebec: CEGEP John Abbot College, Research and Development Secretariat, 1988.

Goleman, Daniel, Boyatzis, Richard E. and McKee, Annie. *Primal Leadership: Learning To Lead With Emotional Intelligence*. Boston, MA: Harvard Business Press, 2012.

Greenleaf, Robert K. and Spears, Larry C. *Servant Leadership: A Journey into the Nature of Legitimate Power and Greatness* (25th anniversary edition). Mahwah, NJ: Paulist Press, 2002.

Greenman, Jeffrey P., Larsen, Timothy, and Spencer, Stephen R. *The Sermon on the Mount through the Centuries*. Grand Rapids, MI: Brazos Press, 2007.

Gyertson, David, Ph.D. "A devoted Christian's view on development of spiritually formed leadership." *International Journal of Spiritual Leadership*, 2007.

Hamel, Mike and Oster, Merrill. "Lead Like Jesus." *Regent Business Review* 10, 2004.

Handler, Charles. (n.d.) "The Value of Person-Organization Fit." *Build an Interview,* Accessed June 2, 2012, http://www.buildaninterview.com/the_value_of_person_organization_fit.asp

Harvard Business Essentials. *Coaching and Mentoring.* HBS Press Book, 2004.

Haslberger, Arno. "Facets and Dimensions of Cross-Cultural Adaptation: Refining the Tools." *Personnel Review* 34, no. 1, 2005: 85-109. doi: 10.1108/00483480510571897

Hassell, David. "Open Communication: Vital to Business Success." *American Management Association*, March 25, 2013, http://www.amanet.org/training/articles/Open-Communication-Vital-to-Business-Success.aspx

Hernez-Broome, Gina and Hughes, Richard L. "Leadership Development: Past, Present, and Future." *Center for Creative Leadership,* n.d.: 27

Hill, Ronald P. and Stephens, Debra L. "The Compassionate Organization in the 21st Century." *Organizational Dynamics* 32, no. 4, 2003: 331-341. doi: 10.1016/j.orgdyn.2003.08.004

Hollo, Diane J. "The Role of Mentorship in Leadership Development and Career Success." Doctoral Dissertation, Carroll University, May 2011.

Hooker, John. "Cultural Differences in Business Communication." *Tepper School of Business*, 2008, http://ba.gsia.cmu.edu/jnh/businesscommunication.pdf

"How Did Business Coaching Get Started?" *Worldwide Association of Business Coaches*, accessed April 14, 2014, http://www.wabccoaches.com/faqs.htm

Huang, Jia-Chi. "Unbundling Task Conflict and Relationship Conflict: The Moderating Role of Team Goal Orientation and Conflict Management." *International Journal of Conflict Management* 21, no. 3, 2010: 334-355. doi: 10.1108/10444061011063207

Hughes, Richard L. and Beatty, Katherine M. *Becoming a Strategic Leader: Your Role in Your Organization's Enduring Success*. San Francisco, CA: Jossey-Bass, 2005.

Hughes, Latanya. "The Borderless Organization." Unpublished Doctoral Paper. Regent University. Virginia Beach, VA, 2013.

Hunt, David Marshall and Michael, Carol. Mentorship: A Career Training and Development Tool. *Academy of Management Review* 8, 1983: 475-485.

Hunter, James C. *The World's Most Powerful Leadership Principle: How to Become a Servant Leader*. Colorado Springs, CO: WaterBrook Press, 2004.

Hutchison, John C. "Servanthood: Jesus' Countercultural Call to Christian Leaders." *Bibliotheca Sacra* 166, 2009: 53-69.

Hybels, Bill. *Who You Are When No One's Looking*. Downers Grove, IL: InterVarsity Press, 1987.

Jackson, Susan E. "Consequences of Group Composition for the Interpersonal Dynamics of Strategic Issue Processing." In Paul Shrivastava, Anne Huff, and Jane Dutton, *Advances in Strategic Management*. Greenwich, CT: JAI Press, 1992.

Jehn, Karen A. "The Impact of Intragroup Conflict on Group Effectiveness: A Multi Method Examination of the Benefits and Detriments of Conflict." Doctoral dissertation, Northwestern University, 1992.

Jenks, Deborah F. "Transformation: An Examination of Jesus' Creative Use of the Matthew 13 Parables and Theory U." School of Global Leadership and Entrepreneurship, Regent University, 2008.

Johnson, W. Brad, and Ridley, Charles R. *The Elements of Mentoring*. New York, NY: PALGRAVE MACMILLAN, 2004.

Kellerman, Barbara. *The End of Leadership*. New York, NY: Harper Business, 2012.

Kram, Kathy E. "Phases of the Mentor Relationship." *The Academy of Management Journal* 26, no. 4, 1983: 608-625.

Kram, Kathy E. *Mentoring at Work: Developmental Relationships in Organizational Life.* Glenview, IL: Scott, Foresman, 1985.

Kraus, Aaron J., and Wilson, Chantale N. "Leadership Development for Organizational Success." *Society for Industrial and Organizational Psychology, Inc.*, 2012.

Kuepers, Wendelin M. "Trans- + -form" Leader- and Followership as an Embodied, Emotional and Aesthetic Practice for Creative Transformation in Organisations. *Leadership and Organization Development Journal* 32, no. 1, 2011: 20-40. doi: 10.1108/01437731111099265

Lamberton, Lowell H. and Minor, Leslie. *Human Relations: Strategies for Success 4th Edition.* Boston, MA: McGraw Hill, 2010.

"Learning Strategies." *University of Kansas Center for Research on Learning*, 2014, http://www.ku-crl.org/sim/strategies.shtml

Leonard, Jonathan S., Levine, David I. and Joshi, Aparna. "Do Birds of a Feather Shop Together? The Effects on Performance of Employees' Similarity with One Another and With Customers," *Journal of Organizational Behavior* 25, no. 6, 2004.

"Likert's Leadership Styles." *Changing Minds,* http://changingminds.org/disciplines/leadership/styles/likert_style.htm

Lockwood, Nancy R. "Workplace Diversity: Leveraging the Power of Difference for Competitive Advantage." *Society for Human Resource Management,* 2005, www.shrm.org/research/quarterly/2005/0605RQuart_essay.asp#f8#f8

Maister, David H., Green, Charles H. and Galford, Robert M. *The Trusted Advisor.* New York, NY: Free Press, 2000.

Malhi, Ranjit S. "Self-Esteem and Peak Performance at Work." *TQM Consultants,* http://www.tqm.com.my/web/05_bookArticle_09.html

"Managing a Multicultural Workforce." *Black Enterprise* 7, 2001: 120.

Maxwell, John C. *The 360º Leader: Developing Your Influence from Anywhere in the Organization.* Nashville, TN: Thomas Nelson, 2005.

Maxwell, John C. *The Complete 101 Collection: What Every Leader Needs To Know.* Nashville, TN: Thomas Nelson, 2009.

Maxwell, John C. "A Leadership Check-Up." *The VOICE Magazine,*

2011, http://www.thevoicemagazine.com/leadership-/leadership/a-leadership-check-up.html

May, Tony. Personal Communication, 2012.

McLeod, Poppy Lauretta, Lobel, Sharon Alisa and Cox, Jr., Taylor H. "Ethnic Diversity and Creativity in Small Groups." *Small Group Research* 27, no. 2, 1996.

McGregor, Jenna. "Why People Really Leave Their Jobs." *Washington Post*, March 18, 2014 http://www.washingtonpost.com/blogs/on-leadership/wp/2014/03/18/why-people-really-leave-their-jobs/

McGuire, David and Hutchings, Kate. "Portrait of a Transformational Leader: The Legacy of Dr. Martin Luther King Jr." *Leadership and Organization Development Journal* 28, no. 2, 2007: 154-166. doi: 10.1108/01437730710726840

McLean, Scott. *Business Communication for Success*. Irvington, NY: Flat World Knowledge, Inc., 2010.

Mellowes, Marilyn. "The Gospel of Matthew: Writing for a Jewish Christian Audience, Matthew's Main Concern Is to Present Jesus as a Teacher Even Greater Than Moses." *Frontline*, 1998, http://www.pbs.org/wgbh/pages/frontline/shows/religion/story/mmmatthew.html June 18

Meltzoff, Andrew N. "Born to Learn: What Infants Learn from Watching Us." PDF document, 1999, http://ilabs.washington.edu/meltzoff/pdf/99Meltzoff_BornToLearn.pdf

Milliken, Frances J. and Martins, Luis L. "Searching for Common Threads: Understanding the Multiple Effects of Diversity in Organizational Groups." *Academy of Management Review* 21, 1996.

Mitchell, Nathan. *Eucharist as a Sacrament of Initiation.* Chicago, IL: Liturgy Training Publications, 1990.

Nanus, Burt. *Visionary Leadership.* San Francisco, CA: Jossey-Bass, 1992.

"National Cultural Dimensions." The Hofstede Centre, http://geert-hofstede.com/national-culture.html

Newberg, Andrew. "Is God Only in Our Brain?" Accessed August 2, 2014, http://www.andrewnewberg.com/research/

Newberg, Andrew. "Do the Temporal Lobes Explain Religious Experiences?" Accessed August 2, 2014, http://www.andrewnewberg.com/research/

Nolan, Albert. *Jesus before Christianity* (Rev. Ed.). Maryknoll, NY: Orbix, 2992.

"Nones on the Rise: One in Five Adults Have No Religious Affiliation." *The Pew Research Center*, October 9, 2012, http://www.pewforum.org/files/2012/10/NonesOnTheRise-full.pdf

Northouse, Peter G. *Leadership: Theory and practice* (4th ed). Thousand Oaks, CA: Sage Publications, 2007.

Obama, Barack. "Presidential Proclamation – National Mentoring Month, 2014." *White House*, December 31, 2013, http://www.whitehouse.gov/the-press-office/2013/12/31/presidential-proclamation-national-mentoring-month-2014

Parolini, Jeanine, Patterson, Kathleen, and Winston, Bruce. "Distinguishing between Transformational and Servant Leadership." *Leadership and organization Development Journal* 30, no. 3, 2009: 274-291. doi: 10.1108/01437730910949544

Pfeffer, Jeffrey. "Working Alone: Whatever Happened To The Idea Of Organizations As Communities?" In James O'Toole and Edward E. Lawler (1st ed), *The New American Workplace*. New York, NY: Palgrave MacMillan, July 29, 2005: 133-138.

Pfeiffer, Charles F., Vox, Howard F., and Rea, John. *Wycliffe Bible Dictionary*. Peabody, MA: Hendrickson Publishers, 2003.

Pirraglia, William. "The Effects of Leadership Styles on the Organization." http://smallbusiness.chron.com/effects-leadership-styles-organization-10387.html

Purkey, William Watson. *Self-Concept and School Achievement.* Englewood Cliffs, NJ: Prentice-Hall, Inc., 1970.

Rahim, M. Afzalur. *Managing Conflict in Organizations.* New York, NY: Praeger Publishers, 1992.

Rinehart, Stacy T. *Upside Down: The Paradox of Servant Leadership.* Colorado Springs, CO: NavPress Publishing Group, 1998.

Robbins, Vernon K. *Exploring the Texture of Texts: A Guide to Socio-Rhetorical Interpretation.* Harrisburg, PA: Trinity Press International, 1996.

Russell, Robert F. "The Role of Values in Servant Leadership." *Leadership and Organization Development Journal* 22, no. 2, 2001: 76-84.

Sarin, Shikhar and McDermott, Christopher. "The Effect of Team Leader Characteristics on Learning, Knowledge Application, and Performance of Cross-Functional New Product Development Teams." *Decision Sciences*, 34, 2003: 707-739. doi: 10.111/j.1540-5414.2003.02350.x

Sayler, Sharon. *What Your Body Says (And How to Master the Message): Inspire, Influence, Build Trust, and Create Lasting Business Relationships.* Hoboken, NJ: John Wiley and Sons, Inc., 2011.

Schaff, Philip. *The Homilies of St. John Chrysostom on Timothy, Titus, and Philemon Nicene and Post-Nicene Fathers* (Vol. 8), Grand Rapids, MI: Christian Classics Ethereal Library, n.d.

Schwartzman, Paul. "Peggielene Bartels: Secretary by Day, King of Otuam, Ghana, by Night." *The Washington Post*, 2009, September 16, http://www.washingtonpost.com/wp-dyn/content/article/2009/09/15/AR2009091503393.html

Scott, Steven K. *The Greatest Man Who Ever Lived: Secrets for Unparalleled Success and Unshakable Happiness from the Life of Jesus.* New York, NY: Doubleday, 2009.

Siebert, Al. *The Resiliency Advantage: Master Change, Thrive Under Pressure, and Bounce Back from Setbacks.* ReadHowYouWant.com, 2009.

"Similarity, community, values and human nature: What about those different folks?" *BATR*. Accessed June 2, 2012. http://www.batr.org/archives/part7.html

Spears, Larry C. "The Understanding and Practice of Servant-Leadership." *School of Leadership Studies Regent University Servant Leadership Research Roundtable*, 2005.

"Stages of intellectual development in children and teenagers." *Child Development Institute*, 1999-2013, http://childdevelopmentinfo.com/child-development/piaget/

Stephens, Hill. "The compassionate organization in the 21st century." *Organizational Dynamics* 32, no. 4, 2003: 331-341. doi: 10.1016/j.orgdyn.2003.08.004

Stone, A. Gregory, Russell, Robert F., and Patterson, Kathleen. "Transformational Versus Servant Leadership: A Difference in Leader Focus." *The Leadership and Organization Development Journal* 25, no. 4, 2004: 349-361. doi: 10.1108/01437730410538671

Strigl, Denny F. *Managers, Can You Hear Me Now?* New York, NY: McGraw-Hill, 2011.

Swindoll, Charles. *Improving Your Serve: The Art of Unselfish Living.* Waco, TX: Word, Incorporated, 1981.

The Lion King. Directed by Rob Minkoff and Roger Allers. 1994. Walt Disney Pictures, Film.

Thomas, David A. and Ely, Robin J. "Making Differences Matter." *Harvard Business Review* 74, no. 5, 1996.

Townsend, John, Ph.D. *Leadership Beyond Reason: How Great Leaders Succeed By Harnessing The Power Of Their Values, Feelings, And Intuition.* Nashville, TN: Thomas Nelson, 2009.

Trevino, Linda Klebe, Brown, Michael and Hartman, Laura Pincus. "A Qualitative Investigation of Perceived

Executive Ethical Leadership: Perceptions from Inside and Outside the Executive Suite," *Human Relations* 56, no. 5: 2003, doi: 10.1177/0018726703056001448

Tutu, Desmond. *No Future without Forgiveness.* New York, NY: Image, 2000.

"Understanding body language." *Psychology Today,* http://www.psychologytoday.com/basics/body-language

US Army Handbook. (1973). *Military Leadership.*

US Department of Justice. "Program Evaluation and Analysis: A Technical Guide for State and Local Governments." Washington, DC: Prepared for the US Department of Housing and Urban Development, 1978.

Vestergaard, Mette. "The Leader is His Own Mentor: Commentary with Mette Vestergaard." *Emerald Group Publishing Limited,* Accessed, August 31, 2011 www.emeraldinsight.com.library.regent.edu/learning/management_thinking/articles/leader_mentor.htm

Ward, Colleen and Kennedy, A. "Crossing Cultures: The Relationship between Psychological and Socio-Cultural Dimensions of Cross-Cultural Adjustment." In Janak Pandey, Durganand Sinha and Dharm P. S. Bhawuk (Eds.), *Asian Contributions to Cross-Cultural Psychology,* New Delhi: Sage Publications, 1996.

Water, Mark. *The Baker Encyclopedia of Bible People: A Comprehensive Who's Who from Aaron to Zurishaddai.* Grand Rapids, MI: Baker Books, 2006.

Westfall, Bill "Leaders Care for the Spirit." *Executive Excellence* 9, 1992.

"What is professional coaching?" *International Coach Federation,* Accessed April 14, 2014, http://www.coachfederation.org/need/landing.cfm?ItemNumber=978andnavItemNumber=567

Wickert, Ulrich. *About The Loss of Values, an Essay.* Hamburg, Germany, 1994.

Wiesel, Elie. "Adolf Hitler." *Time Magazine,* 1998, http://www.time.com/time/magazine/article/0,9171,988156-2,00.html

Wilson, James A., and Elman, Nancy S. "Organizational Benefits of Mentoring." *The Executive* 4, no. 4, 1990: 88-94.

Winston, Bruce. *Be a Leader For God's Sake.* Virginia Beach, VA: School of Leadership Studies, 2002.

Yukl, Gary. *Leadership in Organizations* (4th ed). Upper Saddle River, NJ: Prentice-Hall, Inc., 1998.

Zachary, Lois J. Ed.D. "Group Mentoring: Strategies for Success in Group Mentoring." Retrieved from humanresources.about.com/od/coachingmentoring/a/group_mentoring.htm

Zeffane, Rachid. "Towards a Two-Factory Theory of Interpersonal Trust: A Focus on Trust in Leadership." *International Journal of Commerce and Management* 20, no. 3, 2010. doi: 10.1108/10569211011076938.

About the Author

Dr. Latanya Hughes is an accomplished business professional whose expertise in leadership motivates and inspires audiences to achieve their maximum potential. Her vision is to transform people's lives through positive affirmation. Her philosophy is that it is never too early or too late to change a person's life, improve their leadership skills, or increase their level of influence so they may, in turn, impact nations.

Dr. Hughes holds degrees in Hospitality Management, Business Administration, and Strategic Leadership in Global Consulting. She received her Bachelor's degree from Tuskegee University and her Master's degree from Strayer University. Her Doctoral degree is from Regent University. Connect with Dr. Hughes on Facebook, Google+, and LinkedIn.

Manufactured by Amazon.ca
Bolton, ON

34019295R00162